100 Short Stories and Spiritual Lessons for the Soul

by

Todd Knight

Copyright 2021, Knight Publishing, LLC / authortknight@gmail.com

Table of Contents

INTRODUCTION	3
THE ART OF MANIFESTATION	4
1 IT'S IN GOD'S HANDS	5
2 LESSONS APPLIED	7
3 THE POWER OF THE GENIE WITHIN	9
4 OUR INTENTIONS AND ATTENTION	12
5 OUR GUIDING INTUITION	13
6 HOW TO PRAY	15
7 OUR COLLECTIVE FREE WILL	17
8 OBSERVE THE POWER OF THE MATRIX	18
9 FINDING THE PATH THROUGH PRAYER	19
10 THIS IS NOT HOW MY STORY GOES	21
11 PRAYERS NOT MEANT TO BE ANSWERED	22
12 FOCUS ON THE JOURNEY, NOT THE END	23
13 THE GREATER GOOD	25
14 BE CAREFUL WHAT YOU MANIFEST	26
15 THE ABILITY TO MANIFEST "ANYTHING"	27
16 TO MANIFEST WE MUST LET GO	29
17 THE ART OF NEUTRALITY	30
18 THE POWER OF THE CREATOR	31
19 WITH LOVING INTENT, HELP WILL ARRIVE	33
20 THE COST OF FREE-WILL	35
OUR SOUL'S JOURNEY	36
21 OUR SOUL'S CONTRACT	37
22 WHAT IS A SIN?	38
23 OUR LIFE REVIEW	39
24 RIPPING UP A SOUL'S CONTRACT	41
25 WE ARE NEVER ALONE	43
26 THE GOLDEN RULE	45
27 THE ACCEPTANCE OF DEATH	48
28 OUR CONNECTION TO THE SPIRIT WORLD	49
29 GO INTO THE LIGHT	51
30 A MESSAGE FROM THE SPIRIT WORLD	53
31 A PAST LIFE REMEMBERED	55
32 THE GRAND ASCENSION	56

33	HEAVEN AND HELL ON EARTH	57
34	THE CORRECT PATH IS NOT ALWAYS CLEAR	59
35	INTENTIONS MATTER	60
36	WORKING WITH YOUR SOUL GROUP	61
37	KARMA AND INTENTIONS	63
38	KNOW WHAT IS AT RISK	65
39	THE BRAVEST OF SOULS	67
40	THE LAW OF CONNECTIONS	68

MASTERING THE MIND — 69

41	LEAD WITH STRATEGY NOT EMOTIONS	71
42	THE POWER OF "I AM"	73
43	THE POWER OF APPRECIATION	74
44	DON'T SWEAT THE SMALL STUFF	75
45	BE IN THE MOMENT	77
46	CAN'T HATE OURSELVES INTO CHANGE	78
47	THE DAMAGE CAUSED BY ANGER	79
48	THE DAMAGE CAUSED BY FEAR	81
49	NEVER BE EMBARRASSED	82
50	THE NOTHING TO FEAR BUT FEAR ITSELF	83
51	TIME TO PUT DOWN YOUR WEAPONS	85
52	BE MINDFUL OF YOUR FEAR	86
53	EVERYTHING IS FINE IN THIS MOMENT	87
54	LIVE EVERY DAY LIKE IT'S YOUR LAST	89
55	THE ENTERAL OPTIMIST	90
56	BE BRAVE	91
57	OUR FLEETING EMOTIONS	93
58	BE MINDFUL OF YOUR THOUGHTS	94
59	FOCUS ON THE POSITIVES	95
60	USING APPRECIATION TO HEAL	96

SPIRITUAL WELL-BEING — 97

61	WALK OUR OWN PATH	99
62	THE LAW OF NON-INTERFERENCE	101
63	TEACHER OR STUDENT	102
64	STAND YOUR GROUND	103
65	WE NEED TO FEEL IN ORDER TO HEAL	105
66	THEY DON'T HATE ME	106
67	THE PROCESS OF ELIMINATION	107

68	CHANGES THROUGH SUBSTITUTIONS	109
69	THE KEY TO A LONG-TERM RELATIONSHIP	110
70	THE POWER OF SILENCE	111
71	IT ALL BEGINS WITH OUR CHOICES	113
72	DO WHAT'S RIGHT	114
73	CANCEL CULTURE	115
74	LIFE'S GROWING PAINS	117
75	THAT COULD BE ME	118
76	DO THE DIFFICULT STUFF FIRST	119
77	WE ARE NOT DEFINED BY OUR PAST	121
78	THE CHOICE IS UP TO YOU	123
79	EMBRACE YOUR MISTAKES	124
80	THE TEMPTATION TO MEASURE DAILY ENLIGHTENMENT	125 127
81	STAY PEACEFULL IN THE FLOWING WATER	129
82	THE HEAVENS WILL PROVIDE	131
83	THE LIGHT WITHIN	132
84	PAYING ATTENTION TO THE PUZZLE PIECES	133
85	INTERPRETING THE SIGNS	135
86	ANSWERS AWAIT YOU IN YOUR DREAMS	137
87	EVERYTHING IS BEAUTIFUL ENERGY	138
88	YOUR HIGHEST PROTECTOR	139
89	SEEING REPEATING NUMBERS	141
90	THE DISARMING POWER OF LOVE	143
91	OPENING YOUR THIRD EYE	145
92	YOU ARE THE DIRECTOR OF YOUR LIFE	148
93	ALWAYS PRAY FOR THE TRUTH	149
94	SHARING THE TRUTH	151
95	OUR GREATEST TEACHERS	152
96	WANTING OTHERS TO BEHAVE	153
97	DOES THIS STILL SERVE ME?	155
98	CHOOSE WITH A PEACEFUL HEART	156
99	THE POWER OF INNOCENCE	157
100	THE LESSON OF A SAMURAI	159
THE END		161

Introduction

Our life is like a play that is ever unfolding. Each day, a new scene meant to provide or build upon an important lesson. Each lesson, taught to us through an ever-changing cast of characters. Within this life, we experience several profound moments of spiritual growth. Moments that change our very perception of the world and our place within it. This book is about those moments.

Within the pages to follow are 100 short stories providing a daily dose of inspiration, self-reflection, and spiritual growth.

Each story, represented by its own chapter, is separated into five underlying themes:

Chapters 01 – 20: The Art of Manifestation

Chapters 21 – 40: Our Soul's Journey

Chapters 41 – 60: The Practice of Mindfulness

Chapters 61 – 80: Spiritual Well-Being

Chapters 81 – 100: Enlightenment

The search for spirituality is the search for one's own truth.

The Art of Manifestation

Surrender the path to God and keep moving forward.

We are all co-creators on this Earth, limited in our manifestations by the collective free-will of others.

The question isn't if were living in a simulation, we are. The question is, can we understand the rules of this simulation, so that we can better use this knowledge to our advantage?

Maintain your persistency and faith. You are not meant to fail.

The harder we push, the less we achieve.

It's impossible to manifest one's success while at the same time manifesting failure. So, choose wisely where you place your thoughts, your emotions, your intentions, and attention.

"Anything" is possible on this Earth if it is the choice and free-will of the collective.

The moment you stop asking is the moment you will receive.

We manifest simply by choosing inner peace over fear.

To receive, we must simply be that which we desire. No prayer, bartering, or begging is required. Just the act of being and appreciation in receiving.

Stay true to your belief and help will arrive. Be loving in your intent and the path will be clear.

1 It's in God's Hands

A week had passed since Rasheed had last seen any signs of civilization. As he crawled to the top of a hillside he prayed, "Please dear God, please let this be the path home." He pulled his body up and peered over the horizon, "Desert, nothing but more god-forsaken desert." He shook off his disappointment and moved forward in the hot sun. As he reached the top of the next hill, he believed, he trusted, he maintained his faith, but once again, he saw nothing but desert.

Where there was once hope, there was now only despair and crippling fear. With a heavy heart, Rasheed took one last step and then collapsed onto the ground. His body exhausted. His last amount of goodwill spent. With his forehead pressed against the scorching hot sand he cried out, "Why have you forsaken me? I believed in you. I put my faith in you and you have abandoned me? Why, God, why?"

His body sat motionless under the hot sun until the evening finally came and darkness fell over the horizon. As it did, the pain of the blistering heat finally began to ease. It was just enough relief for him to finally begin to breathe again. Just enough for him to gather his thoughts. Speaking softly to himself he said, "I'm not going to die. I don't know how I know this, but I'm not going to die."

With his last bit of energy, Rasheed rolled over unto his back and stared up at the stars. The cool evening breeze felt good against his sunburn face. For the first time his mind was empty of all thoughts. There were no prayers, no bargaining, just silence and the stars above. Rasheed calmly spoke to himself again, "It's too painful to just sit here. I have no choice but to move forward... Why am walking during the day and resting at night? I have to get out of the sun. From now on, I'm going to find shade during the day..."

Rasheed rolled over onto his chest, "Time to get up. I know that God has heard my prayers. It's up to me now." Rasheed stood up and began to walk. The desert was so dark that night that he wasn't even sure what direction he was headed. But it didn't matter, all that he knew was that he had to keep moving forward. Stumbling ahead, Rasheed reached the top of another hill. As he gathered his breath, he noticed a colorful cluster of stars rising up from the horizon. Then he realized, "Those aren't stars! That's a city! It's far away, but that's a city!" Rasheed fell to his knees and began to cry in relief, "Thank you, God! Thank you for saving my life. Thank you for guiding me on this journey."

Surrender the path to God and keep moving forward.

It was only when Rasheed fully surrendered that his path to salvation became clear. There was no need to beg. No need to barter. His intentions were clear. Now all that he had to do was to fully surrender, to have faith, and to keep moving forward.

2 Lessons Applied

Rasheed had survived his 100-mile journey through the hot sun and had learned many lessons along the way. Vowing to spend the rest of his life as far away from the desert as possible, he joined the Merchant Marines where he ran a small crew that serviced large freighter ships. As fate would have it, Rasheed found himself a few years later stranded out at sea on a small boat with four of his men.

A crew member yelled out, "Look at our fearless leader everyone. We're all stuck out here wet and freezing, and he's acting like he doesn't have a care in the world." Rasheed laughed at the young man and replied, "Trust me, it always could be worse." "Are you kidding me? We're all going to die out here. How could it be worse?" Rasheed calmly replied, "Yes, it's cold and rainy, but your body's not cooking in the hot sun, is it? Trust me, that's worse. And how can you say that we're going to die? We've only been out here for a few days. Don't you have any faith son?" "Faith in who, God? He's the reason we're out here in the first place." Rasheed smiled and replied, "Maybe so, but if he put us here it must have been for a good reason."

After several more days out at sea a crew member yelled out, "We're going to starve to death! Where's your God now? Why won't he help us?" Rasheed understanding the man's frustration leaned forward to comfort his men, "I don't know how, but I know that we're going to survive this. I've survived much worse, and what I've learned is that you have to have faith. You have to trust in God and keep moving forward. Don't worry about how and when we're going to get rescued. Instead, let's focus on how we're going to survive today, agreed?" The men shook their heads in exhaustion. "What do we have to catch fish?" "Nothing! Can't you see we have nothing!" "Terry, if you say one more negative word, I swear we are going to eat you first." The men laughed as they pushed Terry back down in his seat. "John how did you make that bracelet?" "This? I made it from the loose strands from my jacket." "If we all pitched in, do you think you could weave a small fishing line?" "Yeah, I don't see why not."

Before long, John had woven a long fishing line, while the others fashioned a hook and some bait. By the next day, Rasheed's crew had full bellies and in were in good spirits. A week later, a scout on one of the freighter ships heard Rasheed and his men signing off in the distance. "Captain, I hear them! The missing crew, listen, that's them!"

Rasheed and his crew all cheered as they boarded the ship. The captain greeted them with a huge smile, "I can't believe it. You were out there for three weeks. How did you survive?" "Faith," Terry yelled out. "Teamwork," said John. Rasheed extending his hand to the captain, "And lots and lots of fishing."

There is no suffering without meaning, no challenge that lacks importance, no victory without purpose. Every lesson learned is in preparation for the next. Each a vital step along our journey.

3 The Power of the Genie Within

After years of searching in the desert, the young prince found the lost treasure buried deep within the cave. But it wasn't the treasure he was after. It was a golden lamp that held a powerful genie inside. The prince pulled from his pocket a silk scarf that had been hand stitched by his mother. He dropped to his knees as if to pray and rubbed the lamp with the scarf three times.

Heavy smoke began to billow from the lamp temporarily blinding the prince from his men. "You have released me my young prince and for that I am in your debt." A handsome tall man dressed in an elegant blue garment appeared from the smoke. "What is your wish my son, for I will grant the three."

The young prince smiled, "I know of your trickery evil genie. For if I wish for wealth, you will punish me with a great ailment. And if I wish for health, you will banish me to live a life of isolation and solitude." "Ah, I see, you are wise in years. But it is not I, but the wisher, who chooses their path." The young prince shook his head in disbelief, "Once again, you attempt to deceive me. For why would one wish harm upon themselves?"

"No wish for harm, young prince, but simply to replace one gift of knowledge for another." "What gifts do you speak of?" "Wealth, for example, is only an illusion. For wealth cannot buy peace and happiness. And no treasure can be taken to the spirit world." "Still, you say, one chooses to suffer?" "No, the soul chooses to learn. For poverty caries a great many lessons. And if one chooses to wish these lessons away, then new lessons must be put in their place."

The young prince stared at the lantern as he carefully chose his words. "You say then that a wish that is unearned is a gift of knowledge that is given away?" The genie responded with immense pleasure, "You are truly wise, my prince." "Then it is knowledge that I ask for in return for your freedom." "Yes, it is agreed. What knowledge do you wish to possess?" "How do you summon your great powers?" "You mean the power to create?" "Yes, genie. I want to have the power to create."

The genie smiled and bent down to speak softly to the prince, "You already have this power, great prince. The power to create is within us all." "Show me!" the prince snapped back. "Show me how to create."

The genie stepped back to begin his lesson, "Men throughout the ages have searched for this cave, how is it that you were able to find it?" "Through my determination and hard work." "And when did you know that you would succeed." "I've always known. I've never had a doubt." "And here you sit today, with your wish to find me granted. No lessons lost. No gifts of knowledge given away. You manifested this wish, by simply being that which you desire."

The young prince stood up in frustration, "If you continue to try to deceive me, I will return you to your prison and bury you deep beneath the sand." "Deceive you, my prince?" "I desire a great many things, but few of these wishes have come true." "Ah," said the genie, "I see." "See what?" "That you confuse desire with being. For we all want a great many things, but desire is not creating. Desire is simply the yearning for that which we do not have."

The prince standing tall in his anger shouted out, "I will only ask you one more time. How do I create that which I desire?" The genie calmly replied, "By not desiring, but by being." "Nonsense," the prince yelled back. "Tell me young prince, what is it that you desire?" "To rule this land free of my enemies so that my people can live in peace." "Ah! Now that is a noble desire indeed. And so, let us grant you this wish."

The genie continued to speak as he slowly backed away into the fog, "From this moment forward you will rule this land in peace and protection from your enemies. When they attack, you will defend, but not retaliate. Instead of war, you will train your army in agriculture and construction. And when your land grows wealthy and prosperous, you will form an economic partnership with your rivals."

As the genie faded into the fog, "Keep in mind young prince, your patience will be tested. Your resolve, pushed to its limits. But you are a ruler who rules in peace, so a peaceful solution you will always find. And for your noble intent to find peace and harmony in this world, you and your countrymen will be truly blessed and peace you will find." The genie's voice now heard far off in the distance, "Go my young prince and be that which you desire. For your wish has been granted and a great king you will be."

We have the ability to wish away our lessons, but these lessons must be eventually learned. For the harder we resist our chosen path, the more difficult the road will be.

4 Our Intentions and Attention

A woman died and went to the spirit world. Before she returned, her guide taught her one simple lesson. "To manifest your desires, all you need to do is to focus your intentions and attention."

Upon her return, the woman began to manifest her desires. My intention she thought, this is the easy part. "Universe, pay attention! I need a new car. So, I am going to manifest a cute little powder blue sports car. I'll leave the details of how and when, up to you." Attention, now that's the tricky part. I know I'm not supposed to obsess about my new car. So how do I put my attention toward something without driving my guardian angels crazy? Looking up at the sky, "Well angles, how should I give this matter my attention?"

Later that day, the woman drove past the motor vehicle department. "Thanks for the reminder, I'll need to register my new car soon." At the stop light she came upon a bright blue jeep. "That's a pretty blue, but I'm looking for something more in a powder blue." The car next to her backfired while smoke poured out of its muffler. "Oh, and if I forgot to mention it, thank you for giving me a car in perfect working condition."

The woman never begged for her car. She didn't obsess over it at every moment. She simply enjoyed the journey, knowing that her dream car would come into her life soon, and it did. A few weeks later, the perfect car, at the perfect price, was put up for sale a few houses down. "There it is! It's perfect! Thank you, my angels."

5 Our Guiding Intuition

There I was, standing in Walmart watching my son contemplate the best way to spend his Christmas money. After what felt like an hour, he turned to me and asked, "How do you choose between two things that you really want?" Putting my arm around his shoulders I said, "Let me show you a great trick. We're going to let your heart decide."

As I pulled a quarter out of my pocket, "We're going to flip a coin. If it comes up tails, then the drone wins, and if it comes up heads, the knife wins. Okay?" "How is that making a decision from my heart?" "You don't have to do what the coin says. What's important, what I want you to pay attention to, is how you feel when you first get the results. Do you feel excited and happy or do you feel a sense of disappointment?"

I flipped the coin high into the air and shouted, "Here we go! Who's going to be the winner?" We both watched with anticipation as it spun around the isle finally settling on heads. Doing my best to seem excited I yelled out, "Heads! The knife wins!"

As I started to put the drone back on the shelf, I noticed the wheels spinning in my son's head. "Well, how do you feel? Are you excited?" "To be honest, no, I'm not." I looked at him and said, "That's great! Now you know your answer. Your gut, your intuition, your heart, it's telling you what you really want. You want the drone, right?" After a moment of reflection, he smiled and shook his head, "Yeah! I want the drone."

I placed the knife back on the shelf and handed him the drone. "How you do you feel now?" "Really good," he said. "Me too. Remember, whenever you're making a crucial decision, always do a gut check first." Pointing to my son's chest, "Trust your heart, it will always tell you the truth."

There the answer was, so clear, so unmistakable in its response. All that I had to do was to quite my mind, and to feel my heart.

If we learn nothing else in this life, we must learn to trust how we feel. This is our intuition, our voice to God, our voice to our higher selves. It speaks to us at all times. It guides us down the correct path and warns us of trouble ahead. Trust in your intuition because there is nothing in this universe that loves you more than God, your angels, and your higher soul.

6 How to Pray

I once asked an extremely gifted psychic and spiritual coach, "If there is one thing that you could teach someone, what would it be?" She responded, "I would teach them how to pray. The practice of prayer is so important, yet most of us don't know how to pray."

She continued, "It doesn't matter who you pray to or how you pray. You can pray to your higher self, your guardian angels, Jesus, Allah... It doesn't matter, it's all the same divine power."

"What's important, is that is that we do the following three things when we pray. The first, is to ask for something that we truly believe that we are worthy of receiving. Something of loving intent that will in no way negatively affect others. The second, is to know in our hearts that we are deserved of this thing that we are asking for and that God will provide it to us. And then finally, we must let go and have faith in God's timing."

I responded, "This sounds very similar to the law of attraction; ask, believe, and receive." "It is!" she replied. "It's exactly the same. You see there is only one truth. It's wrapped up in different faiths and religions, but it's all the same truth. The mistake that we make is believing that our version of the truth is the only one that's correct."

I then asked, "Why do you think that most people have a tough time praying?" "They don't know how to let go and to trust in God's timing. Asking is the easy part. Even believing that we are worthy, that's easy too. But letting go and trusting in God's timing, that is the difficult part for all of us."

She continued, "What we tend to do is to pray for something that we believe we need or want and then as time passes, we unintentionally flood our thoughts with doubt and worry." "I know," I replied. "It seems like our mind is always in contradiction with our soul. So how do we make sure that we don't sabotage ourselves?" "Just pray, "let thy be done." Trust me, God and your angels know you better than you know yourself. They know exactly what you want and exactly what you need. By praying, "Let thy be done," you are not only putting your faith into their hands, but also ensuring that you don't cancel out your prayers with any conflicting thoughts."

I then asked, "Is there anything that we shouldn't pray for?" "Yes!" she replied. "Never pray to inflict harm onto others. This will only result in bad karma for yourself." "So, how then do we pray then for others to stop hurting us?" "Always pray for the truth to be revealed. Put bright light around these people and pray that they learn their lessons and that they understand the truth of their actions. Then put bright light around yourself and ask for God's loving protection."

Ask, believe, and fully let go in order to receive.

7 Our Collective Free Will

Captain Simone Wilson was the first astronaut to walk on Mars. As she took her first steps on the planet's red surface she realized, "We have a lot of work to do." Her mission, along with her crew of 20, was to terraform the planet by melting its icy polar caps. This was a mission that was conceived over ten years ago and one that cost over a trillion dollars to achieve.

As Simone stared out at the horizon, she reflected back on the conversation that she had with her daughter. "I still don't get it! Why would they waste all of this money to terraform a far-off planet when we could just save our own?" "You're not wrong, Jada." "Then why are you going?" "I'm going because it's my job. I'm going because we have to do something before this planet dies."

Jada put her head down and began to cry, "I don't want you to go! Why can't we just fix the Earth?" "You know I have thought about that question a lot, and what it comes down to is our collective free-will." "What does that mean?" "It means for whatever reason, right or wrong, there are more people who want to put up the time and money to terraform Mars than there is to fix the Earth." "That's messed up!" "I know. It's why we got into this mess in the first place. Not enough people want to do the right thing." Simone hugging her daughter, "Trust me, baby. If it where up to me, I'd be right here by your side helping to fix this planet instead of running off to fix Mars."

> *We are all co-creators on this Earth, limited in our manifestations by the collective free-will of others.*

8 Observe The Power of the Matrix

The woman woke from her nap to a blank TV screen. "How odd," she thought, "the sound is playing but the screen is blank." But just then as her eyes began to adjust, the picture on the screen magically appeared. It was if the universe realized, "Oops, she's awake now. Time to turn on the screen."

The next day, the woman enjoyed her favorite music playing through her home's AI device. But when she stepped outside to work in the garden, the music magically paused. Intrigued, she thought to herself, "There is no way this device knew that I went outside. I wonder why it paused the music?"

The question isn't if we're living in a simulation, we are. The question is, can we understand the rules of this simulation, so that we can better use this knowledge to our advantage?

The most powerful proof of manifestation may be found in the study of quantum physics. For studies have shown that an atom's structure maintains a fluctuating and undermined state of energy until it is observed. Put more simply, matter does not exist until it is created through our observation.

So, what do you observe? A world of pain and suffering? Then this is what will manifest into your existence.

Instead, observe the glory of this world. Observe your strength and power. Observe your happiness and joy. Your good health and abundance. Observe all of the things that you want to attract, and the matrix, this simulation that you control, will have no choice but to deliver.

9 Finding the Path Through Prayer

Eric was having another sleepless night worrying about the bills. "This money is going to run out soon. Then what am I going to do? How am I going to feed my kids? Who's going to put a roof over our heads?"

Trying to fall asleep, he reached for a bottle of whiskey hidden underneath the bed. After filling his glass, he lowered his head and began to cry, "God, why can't you help me? Please! Just tell me what to do. I'll do whatever you want. I just need you to guide me. I just need you to show me the way."

At that moment, his daughter walked into the room. Eric startled, picked up his glass and walked to the kitchen. Out of embarrassment, he quickly poured the drink down the sink. "You okay daddy?" "Yeah baby, I was just cleaning up."

The next morning, feeling a little better, Eric sat down and enjoyed his morning coffee. "What the hell am I doing with all of this debt? I have two vehicles and a motorcycle. That's just stupid. I need get rid of some of this stuff."

Leaning back in his chair, "Who cares that the plant didn't hire me. I don't know how, but I'm going to get that job. I'm the perfect fit for that company, they just don't know it yet." As he took another big sip of coffee, "You know what? I'm going to apply for that position every single month until they hire me or tell me to go away. What do I have to lose? The worst case, they'll know I'm persistent."

After applying for the same job, for the third month in a row, Eric was contacted by the plant's human resources department. "You know we rarely have an opening in that department, but if we do, we will certainly keep you in mind. "That's what I thought," Eric replied. "I appreciate the call." "That's not why I was calling. I see here on your application that you're an experienced welder." "Yes, I've done welding work for the past ten years." "I was curious why you haven't applied for one of our welding positions? It's a day shift, which most people prefer, and the pay is considerably higher." Eric in shock quickly responded, "A welding job? That would be perfect!"

Maintain your persistency and faith. You are not meant to fail.

We are not meant to suffer, and we are not meant to fail. There is only our resistance to our lessons and our unwillingness to ask for help. Will the answers always be clear and sudden? No. But if we ask for guidance, accept the truth, and stay the course, help will always be provided, and salvation will always be ahead.

10 This is Not How My Story Goes

A father in a panic pushed his way through a large crowd. "SAMANTHA! he yelled out. "Samantha where are you!?" As he passed an elderly couple he asked, "Have you seen a little girl in a blue dress?" Tears began to roll down his face as they shook their heads no. "Oh my God, I just turned my back for one second. She has to be here."

The man fell to his knees and began to pray, "I can't lose my little girl. God, you have to help me. Please help me find her." Just then, as the man began to catch his breath, he had a moment of clarity. "This is not how my story goes." Feeling somewhat better, he repeated it to himself, "This is not how my story goes. I don't lose my daughter. I am going to find her. I know that she is safe."

The man took a deep breath and wiped away his tears. "Sir, have you seen a little girl? How about you sir, have you seen a girl in a blue dress?" The man yelled out into the crowd, "HAS ANYONE SEEN A LITTLE GIRL IN A BLUE DRESS?" A voice responded off in the distance, "She's over here. She's with the police officer by the ticket booth."

Have faith in your higher-soul and the life that you have chosen. Your path, never too dark. Your limitations, always known.

When life is at its worst, ask yourself, "Is this really how my story goes?" Would I really choose such a dark and painful path? If not, take a deep breath and get back on track. Remember, you are never set up to fail. Your purpose, always to experience and learn.

11 Prayers Not Meant to Be Answered

I remember as a young man passionately praying that my soon-to-be ex-girlfriend would change her mind about breaking up with me. At that moment, I truly believed that her choice would determine if I would ever be happy again. But I soon came to realize that it wasn't her who causing the pain at all. It was my own intuition screaming out, "Let her go! She is not the one!" And when I finally did, this dreadful pain that I felt in my heart immediately went away.

My prayers on that day were not meant to be answered. My intuition, that pain in my heart, this was my higher soul's response to my request. It was leveraging its most powerful tool, my emotions, to guide down the right path. "Let go of her," my intuition screamed. "Be appreciative of the time that you had together and move on. Yes, she is wonderful, but no, she is not the one."

Your intuition is always talking to you. The more you ignore it, the more painful things will become.

If we knew our own powers, if we knew who we actually were, we would simply manifest our way out of every tricky situation. But then, what would be the point of this difficult life? This veil that blinds us to who we are, is by our own design. Its purpose is to stop us from manifesting literally "anything" we desire. Only when we are limited in our powers can we truly embrace these challenging experiences so that we can learn our lessons.

12 Focus on the Journey, Not the End

Jacob was a man with lofty ambitions. He graduated from the top of his class and now was on the fast track to a long and successful career. Like many people his age, Jacob had an extensive list of goals that he wanted to accomplish during his life. He wanted to get married, to have lots of kids, to buy a large house, and to become a manager within a major company, all before his 30th birthday.

These were his goals and nothing was going to get in his way. When he interviewed for a job, he wanted to know how quickly he could rise through the ranks. When he went on a date, he would ask about their intentions to get married and have kids. Every action he took, every habit formed, was with a focused intent to achieve his goals.

To Jacob's surprise, by the time he had reached his 30th birthday, he had hardly accomplished a single goal. When selecting a job, he chose the company that would provide the greatest upward mobility. But later he admitted, "This place is horrible. Now I know why it's so easy to get promoted here, everyone is either quitting or getting fired." And regarding his love life, most of the girls he dated just wanted to have fun and were often put-off by his eager attempts to get married.

Everything that Jacob had been taught about setting aggressive goals seemed to fail. And so, he decided on his birthday that he was done. "I've waisted my twenties chasing these ridiculous goals and I'm no closer to them then when I started. From now on I'm just going to relax and enjoy my life."

Once Jacob made this decision everything began to change. He excelled at his job. Not because of his goal to succeed, but because he embraced his position and took joy in his work. He found a new love. Not because he was in search for a wife, but because he relaxed and enjoyed the company of a new friend. His newfound success, he realized, was not because he had abandoned his goals. Far from it. It was because his focused had shifted from the end goal to the joyous journey.

The harder we push, the less we achieve.

It's important that we express ourselves though our choices and ambitions and that we set our intentions and attention toward the things that we desire. But ironically, the harder we strive toward a chosen goal, the less likely we are to achieve it. Remember, it's never about the act of wanting, but always about the intent of being. Being that very thing that you desire, the person that you want to be, that thing you want to achieve.

13 The Greater Good

Some say that Gary has been an entrepreneur from birth. When most kids were setting up a lemonade stand, Gary had a full-blown kitchen with peanut butter sandwiches and "vanilla and chocolate" milk. By the time he reached his 50th birthday, Gary had opened and ran over thirty businesses. Some of them were extremely successful, and some, colossal failures. His daughter, the only child to follow him in the business, once asked, "How do you know if a business is going to succeed or fail?"

He responded, "There are many ways that you can ensure that a business will do well. You start with a good business plan. Have plenty of funding. A solid product that is in demand..." "Well then, why have so many of your business failed?" "Ah! Because it took me most of my life to learn what's most important about starting any new business, and that is, it must serve the greater good." "I don't understand, didn't all of your businesses serve the greater good?" "Not necessarily. I definitely thought that they would all be profitable, but I learned, profitability alone does not make a successful business." "For example?" "I figured out a way to buy concert tickets in advance at a huge discount. The idea was that I would resell them at a hefty premium. It was a great idea that made a lot of financial sense, especially for me, but it was a huge failure." "Why?" "Because the only object was for me to make money. And because a competitor can always offer a lower price. If you want the wind at your back and the universes by your side, make sure your work is always for the greater good. If you do this, you will rarely fail at whatever you do."

14 Be Careful What you Manifest

A man was asked to read his letter to a large crowd. The letter stated that for several years the man tried his best to implement the laws of attraction but instead of his life getting better it had only become worse. The letter went on to share the man's long-held intention to confront the speaker about her false teachings and to read this letter of disappointment to her audience. He concluded, "It was only through my determination and persistency that I made it to the stage here today." The man shouted as he stormed out of the room, "The law of attraction, manifestation, it's all a lie!"

It's impossible to manifest one's success while at the same time manifesting failure. So, choose wisely where you place your thoughts, your emotions, your intentions, and attention.

What the man didn't realize is that he unintentionally provided the audience with an excellent example of manifestation. The man chose this action, he visualized it, he placed emotion around it. He was persistent in his intentions and attention until he eventually he manifested himself unto that stage. It worked! The confusion is that one can only manifest positive events into their life. This of course is not the case at all. If you think about it, visualize it, and place emotion (vibration) toward a negative event, you will manifest this event. This is why it is so important to be mindful of our thoughts and emotions. Remember, you are always manifesting. You are always drawing in what you think and feel.

15 The Ability to Manifest "Anything"

Treavor tried to manifest a specific job at his dream company, to work alongside Karri, his dream girl. Frustrated by his lack of progress, he visited a spiritual advisor to receive some guidance. "I don't understand. I thought I could manifest "anything" but I'm no closer to getting this job than I was a year ago. What am I doing wrong?" "Maybe nothing," she replied. "This may just be God's timing. But before we decide, let's first consider the intentions of your manifestation." "The intentions?"

"You certainly have the free will to manifest anything that you want. The question is, will this manifestation serve your best interests and the best interests of others?" "Of course, it will, this is my dream job working alongside my dream girl." "Yes, but remember, you are a co-creator on this Earth. Every soul, just like yours, has free will. I'm sure Karri is a very special girl, but you can't manifest her love for you. This has to be given out of free will. Similar to the job, you can't manifest that a manager hires you over someone who may be better suited. This also must be given out of free will."

"I get the girl part, but are you saying I can't manifest my dream job?" "Of course, you can. But you may not be able to manifest that specific job with that specific company. Instead, you should manifest that you will find both your dream job and true love in the near future. Remember, the more specific your manifestation, the more challenging you make it for the universe to deliver."

"I'm confused, I thought I was supposed to be very specific with my manifestations." "Visualization is just a tool to help tune your emotions. You visualize yourself doing the task of your dream job. Then more importantly, you feel the satisfaction and joy that this position would provide. Specifics in timing, people, actions that you hope that they will take on your behalf... All of these things can cloud your emotions and slow your manifestation."

"Anything" is possible on this Earth if it is the choice and free-will of the collective.

We are all co-creators on this Earth, and we all are blessed with free-will. Manifestation, therefore, can be limited by the free-will of the collective. You alone cannot manifest world peace, only the peace that you find within yourself. You can't manifest the love of another, only that you will find true love.

What you can manifest, without limitation, is your experience in this world. How you react, the choices you make, the free-will that you exercise. This is the "anything' that is possible. This is what has no limitations.

16 To Manifest We Must Let Go

I came across an exercise where you try to manifest a single blue within 48 hours. I didn't think much about it until the next morning when I came across a blue feather sitting in solitude on my living room floor. "Wow," I thought to myself. "Why aren't all of my manifestations this quick and easy?"

When we struggle to attract the things we desire, we often ask ourselves; Am I constantly changing my mind? Is my request too specific? Are my negative thoughts and emotions canceling out my prayers? Down deep, do I believe that I'm worthy? Is what I'm trying to manifest in conflict with my soul's contract? Will it help me but harm others? Do I need to complete an important lesson first? But regardless of your answers, please always know, you're not doing anything wrong, you're simply remembering how to do it right.

The moment you stop asking is the moment you will receive.

Of all the things that we can do to improve our ability to manifest our desires, by far the most difficult and often the most important, is to let go and to have faith in God's timing. For it's often the emotion and the heavy vibration of desire that repels the very thing that were trying to attract.

17 THE ART OF NEUTRALITY

Aziz spent the morning meditating and visualizing his dream home. Through much practice, he mastered the emotional state that he thought was needed in order to manifest this house, a state of bliss as if a white light enveloped every part of his being. He saw it, he felt it, this house must surely manifest.

The next day Aziz received some unwelcome news. He had lost his job due to no fault of his own and would now have to find a way to feed his family. "How am I supposed to feel bliss now?" he asked himself. "All I feel now is worried and concerned. I'll put aside my desire for a new house for a while and just concentrate on finding a new job."

The next few months were difficult for Aziz but as tempted as he was, he never embraced the emotion of fear. Instead, he did his very best to stay calm, to stay emotionally neutral. He said to himself, "I may not be able to manifest my dream home, but I sure don't want to manifest anything bad into my life."

As time passed, Aziz's situation slowly improved. It wasn't long before he found a better job, and eventually, a better house. He thought to himself, "How could this be? I didn't maintain the emotional bliss needed to manifest this beautiful home." But then he remembered, when we are faced with challenges in our life. When fear and doubt are clear emotional choices. Simply choosing emotional neutrality, keeping a state of inner peace during a challenging time, this is the equivalent of maintaining emotional bliss.

We manifest simply by choosing inner peace over fear.

18 The Power of the Creator

A great wizard stood silent on the edge of the forest. "What great magic do you share with us today?" a tribesperson yelled out. "The power of the light," the wizard responded. "God's golden light?" "Yes!" The wizard pointed to his chest, "It is within us all. Right here. This light... it gives us the power to create. The power to heal."

"Can we use this light to crush our enemies?" "No," the wizard replied. "The light can only be used to create, not to destroy." "Can it be used to bend the will of man?" "No, for each man has his own free-will." "Then what good is this light?" the tribal leader shouted. "For what can be created, will surely be destroyed."

"Destroyed?" said the wizard. "What can be destroyed? Livestock, grain, a piece of land? Do not limit your view to this world, to this short life. For God's light is internal, and so is your soul." The tribal leader stood tall to speak, "We believe you great wizard but it's today that we must eat. It's today that we seek shelter from our enemy. How can God's light help us to survive this very day?"

"Through the power of creation," the wizard replied. "If it is food that we need. Then food will be provided. If it is shelter that we seek. Then God will show us the way. We can use God's light to ensure our own salvation, but never at the cost of our enemies' demise."

"Show us then, show us how to use this magical light. Show us how to call upon its great powers." The wizard smiled and looked upon the group, "It's easier than you might think. For there is no prayer that is needed. No sacrifice that must be made. It is all a matter of intent and being."

The wizard, sensing the tribespeople confusion yelled out, "Is it our intent to be well fed?" "Yes!' the tribespeople cheered. Then from now on it is agreed. We will be well fed. But in order to receive this great gift, we must all act in a manner of those who are well fed. We will hunt often. We will gather daily. And we will show our appreciation for this abundance through our daily prayer."

"But first, we must all agree... Not one of us will speak or act as if we are hungry ever again. For those who speak of hunger, only attract the desire for food."

"So, how do we eat today?" a tribe member yelled out. "What are the actions of a man who is well fed?" the wizard replied. "Does he ask who will feed him or does he take action to feed himself?" The tribe member reflected upon the question as the wizard continued, "Get up my friend. Get up and act. For you are a man who is well fed, and a man who is well fed has much to do."

To receive, we must simply be that which we desire. No prayer, bartering, or begging is required. Just the act of being and appreciation in receiving.

19 With Loving Intent, Help Will Arrive

A daughter pleads with her mother, "PLEASE! Do not send this man $10,000. This is a scam!" "No, it's not! Fernando is a real person and we are in love." "Mom, you're almost 80 years old. There is no handsome doctor who's stationed in Syria who is about to retire and move to Kentucky with you." "Can't you just be happy for me?" "Of course, but this is not real!" "Well, you're just going to have to trust me."

The daughter searched the web for the doctor's name. "Look! They're using this guy's picture to rip people off." "I know, he told me that people have been using his pictures." The daughter completely frustrated, "Are you serious? Look for yourself. After seeing this, you still think you're dating the real doctor?" "Yes, I do, and you'll meet him this Wednesday when he arrives from Syria."

"Why does a successful doctor need you to wire him $10,000?" "He needs it in order to buy himself out of the country." "To buy himself off an army base... Where he's a doctor?" "Yes!" The daughter began to cry. "I don't understand." "What?" the mother replied in a stern voice. "How you have become so gullible, so venerable?" "So stupid? Is that what you want to say?" "Well yes, but I'm not here to call you names. I'm here because I love you. I'm here because I want to protect you." "Like I said, you're just going to have to trust me."

The daughter now in a state of shock and terror, "I need the money!" "What? You're just saying that so that I don't send it to him." "No, I swear on my children's life. We need the money. Just as a short-term loan. You know that Bob is in between jobs. Well, we have run out of money and we have no way to pay the bills. I wasn't going to come to you because I didn't think you had it, but $10,000, that is exactly what we need." The mother responded in a concerned voice, "I knew that you and Bob had been struggling. You should have come to me sooner."

The daughter continued, "I honestly believe that God has put us both in the situation so that we could help each other. I know that you believe that you're in love with this man, but I need your help like I've never needed it before. Will you please lend me the money instead of giving it him? If he truly loves you, I'm sure he will understand."

After an extended period of silence, the mother agreed to give her daughter the $10,000. Fernando was infuriated. He sent the mother several nasty texts and screamed at her over the phone. It was then that she finally realized, "This man doesn't love me. No one who loved me would treat me this way. It hurts to admit it, but I see now that this was just a scam."

Stay true to your belief and help will arrive. Be loving in your intent and the path will be clear.

20 The Cost of Free-Will

Millions of light years away a blueish green alien sat bored staring out into space. Its task was to study the planets in the galaxy which hold extraterrestrial life. Its favorite planet? Earth. "What an amazing paradox," it said to itself. "It's one of the most beautiful places in the galaxy, filled with lush vegetation, diverse life, and deep oceans. But the dominate species... what a mess." It wondered, "Is it worth it? Would the freedom to have unlimited free-will be worth it even if it came at the cost of the planet?"

As the alien ended its day, it repeated the same routine that it had for the past hundred years. It consumed the same flavorless liquid for nutrition. It completed the same ceremonial steps as it prepared for rest. As the alien laid to bed that night it knew that it would awake to a world free of crime, war, and hatred. And even knowing the great destruction that these forces have caused on Earth, it still asked itself that night, "Would it be worth it?'

Want to release a massive amount of karmic debt and ascend quickly in the spirt world? Then the Earth is the school for you.

It's a double edge sword, free-will. It's responsible for everything that makes us special as a species and for every reason that we have failed. But that's the point. We are meant to fail. For failure provides the greatest opportunity for growth. This is why it is so important that we fully express ourselves, and that we embrace this luxury which is our free-will. Regardless of your choice, know that it will always be worth it.

Our Soul's Journey

Our fate, our destiny, is the path that we have chosen and the commitments we've made.

We are all watched over with loving care each step of the way.

Through an infinity of time, our soul has reincarnated into every existence and every state of being that has ever been.

In the end, there is only one lesson that matters. Only one commandment that we all must follow.

Celebrate this life. Participate in all of its glory. Stay true to yourself and never worry about the opinions of others.

For those souls who are ready to ascend, the Earth will provide a new home. For others, the opportunity for growth will lay upon another planet.

Be flexible in your journey. What may seem like your destiny, may actually be your demise.

We act in kindness and with love, not for some reward awaiting us in this life or the next, but for the joy and fulfillment that the act itself gives us in this very moment.

We choose our supporting cast of characters. Each with a specific role to play. Each with an important purpose.

Brick by brick, lesson by lesson, each decision effecting the next. Our choices all connected, our past and future, all represented in this very moment.

21 Our Soul's Contract

An angel approaches a soul resting in Heaven, "It's time to continue your lessons. The soul meets with its guides to discuss its next life of on Earth. Like a director of a play, the soul chose its story line, a cast of characters, the time of its birth and death, and most importantly, the events of its life, good and bad, that will help them to learn their lessons.

Keep in mind, the soul when making these decisions is in a state of relative emotional bliss. As a result, it ambitiously adds as many lessons as possible having little understanding of the physical and emotional pain that lay ahead. The soul's advisor, with great concern, attempts to warn the soul of the perilous journey, "This may be too much karmic debt to take on in one lifetime." But the courageous soul insists on moving forward. "Okay then," the guide replied. "We will be here if you need our help." After the soul and its guides complete their extensive planning process, the soul commits to its contract and reincarnates unto the Earth. School is in session.

Our fate, our destiny, is the path that we have chosen and the commitments we've made.

We are never alone in this life. We are not a singular entity walking blindly along a difficult path which leads us to either heaven or hell. Heaven, the spirit world, is the only choice that awaits us. We are not a separate entity, but instead an extension of our higher soul that has chosen to reincarnate unto this Earth, this school, so that we can learn a predetermined set of lessons. This is our soul's contract.

22 What is a Sin?

A preacher crashed his car into a semi-truck and died. His spirit left his body and returned to heaven where he met his guide. "We are so happy to see you, but your work on Earth is not done. Before you return to your body, do you have any questions?" After a moment of thought the preacher asked, "I often feel conflicted about the word of God (the Bible). I wonder, what is a sin?" "That is an excellent question," the guide responded, "and one with the simplest of answers. It's love." "Love?"

"Is guidance given or action taken, done so with loving intent? Love towards oneself or love towards another? If so, then it is a righteous act that is free of sin." The preacher still confused, "So, eating fish on Friday?" "What does that have to do with loving intent?" "The choice of one's religion?" "Is the intent toward finding one's truth? Is it a philosophy based in the respect and care of others? If so, then how could this be considered a sin?"

The preacher later recovering in his hospital bed reflected upon the conversation with his guide, "So simple, yet so profound. Is the act given with loving intent? I will preach from this philosophy from this day forward because I know now that it is the true word of God."

A life lived with loving intentions and loving actions, is a life that is truly worth living.

23 Our Life Review

Wilhelm reincarnated unto this Earth with a purpose to learn the lesson of forgiveness. This was his soul's contract, and the karma he was to release. In a past life, his soul experienced tremendous trauma when a German officer killed his family during the war. Although he tried, he was never able to free himself of the pain of this event and eventually died many years later still holding on to his resentment and anger.

As a young German officer, Wilhelm was considered to be a person of strong morality and kind heart. But these characteristics corrupted by his power as a military officer. As a result, he never completed his soul's contract or learned the lessons that he set out to learn. Instead, his soul left this Earth accumulating new lessons. Lessons that would have to be learned over many lifetimes.

When Wilhelm returned to the spirit world there was no judgement for his actions, no punishment awaiting. The only questioned asked by his spirit guides, "Well, how did you do?" "Not so well," he replied. "Not only did I not learn the lesson of forgiveness, but I see now that I have many lessons yet to learn. Soul Wilhelm continuing to reflect on his life, "And... many souls that I must repay."

In this life and in the next, you will always be your greatest critic. In this life or in the next, you will eventually learn your lessons.

Our souls pass from this Earth and return to the spirit world in the form of pure energy. After a time of rest, we are asked to meet with our guides to conduct two life reviews. The first review is our life as seen through our own eyes. This is meant as a way for us to reflect upon our choices and to determine if we completed our soul's contract.

The second review is from the perspective of those around us. This review is to help us to understand how our actions affected others. How the pain or pleasure we inflicted, intentional or not, rippled throughout the universe. This review is not only as a means to give us a greater perspective to the depth and consequences of our actions, but also to help us to understand how powerful we are as co-creators on this Earth.

At no point during either review are we judged for our actions. There's no punishments or reward awaiting us at the end of our journey. The only question, did we learn our lessons, did we satisfy our soul's contract, or have we accumulated new lessons, new karmic debt to be paid in another life?

24 Ripping Up a Soul's Contract

When Sarah and Bob first married twenty years ago, they both shared a pessimistic view. They would spend hours passionately, and joyfully, discussing how everything in the world was so screwed up. Sarah used to enjoy these conversations and often thought that this was one of the reasons that they got along so well. But as the years passed something began to change. Sarah, exhausted by all the hatred, started to search for new friends and hobbies. She was open to any experience as long as it was positive and it didn't involve politics, conspiracies, or heated debates.

Bob, however become more bitter and angry as the years passed. Sarah, after listening to her husband's nightly rant, finally realized that she had outgrown her soulmate. "He has nothing to offer me now, nothing but hatred and anger. It saddens me to say, but it's time for me to let him go."

As she prayed that night, "Soul Robert, I thank you for our shared time on this Earth. I thank you for the lessons that you have taught me in this life and in the past. I love you. I place bright light around you and I wish you all the best."

Then while visualizing herself ripping up a contract, "It is time for us now to separate. You have so many difficult lessons left ahead. I've been happy to be your teacher in the past, but you would be better served with a new teacher now. With the great love, I rip up our soul's contract and ask that you release me and leave me in peace. Amen, amen, amen."

I release you out of love. I no longer want to share in your painful lessons. A better teacher awaits you now.

A divorce is a contractual agreement limited to this Earth. In order to truly separate from someone, not only in this life but the next, you need to rip up your soul's contract and release them. You can do this this through prayer, meditation, or in a lucid state where one soul speaks directly to another. Do not make this prayer out of anger or with false intentions, for this will only result in more shared lessons. Release them if you're ready but do so with loving intent. The goal never to punish, but always to grow.

25 We Are Never Alone

Christy sat on the same spot, on the same bridge, every day for the past two months. She said to herself as she stared at the rocky bottom below, "If only I had the courage to jump." Wiping the tears from her eyes, "I just want this pain to stop. I don't care what's on the other side. It can't be any worse than this."

She arrived at her home just as the sun began to set. "Where the hell have you been?" "I'm sorry Mamma, I had to walk home again." "Well, I hope you don't think you're getting any dinner. We ate your meal an hour ago." Christy screamed back as she stormed into her room, "I hate my life! I hate everything about it!"

As Christy slept that evening her guardian angels discussed her fate. "You know we are not allowed to interfere." "We are if she intends to end her life." "A nudge, that's all I'm suggesting. An opportunity to explore a different path…" The angels looked over her body with great care, "Then its agreed. A nudge it is."

On the way home the next day, Christy was stopped by a train that was blocking the rails to the bridge ahead. "Can't be late again," she said to herself. "Guess I'll cut through the Bradberry's farm to save some time." As she did, she came across Ms. Bradberry working in her garden. Seeing Christy pass by she yelled out, "Good! You can help me." Christy, a little confused, stopped in her path. Ms. Bradberry yelled out again, "You, come here. I need your opinion."

As Christy reached the edge of the garden, Ms. Bradberry placed a piece of fruit into her hand. "Try this and let me know what you think. Is this a pineberry or a strawberry?" Christy looked down at a white piece of fruit that resembled a strawberry. "It's a strawberry," she replied. "That's what my husband said, but I think it's a pineberry. Taste it. If its ripe then it's a pineberry, if its tart, then it's a strawberry." Christy bashfully put the piece of fruit into her mouth, "It's good. It tastes sweet." "Pineberry!" Ms. Bradberry yelled out, "I knew it."

The next day, Christy took the same path home making sure to stop by the Bradberry's farm. Once again, she was greeted with welcome arms and a loving heart. "There you are, I was hoping that you'd to stop by today. Would you like to try a fresh tomato?" "I sure would," she replied.

Christy never felt alone again. Ms. Bradberry's love and friendship had saved her life. All that she needed was a little nudge from her angels. A little nudge to let her know that life was good and that she was loved.

We are all watched over with loving care each step of the way.

We are never alone. We are all blessed with at least one guardian angel who is with us throughout our entire life. A divine loving entity who deeply cares for us and want's nothing more than to help. Pray to them in your time of need. Speak to them daily and throughout life's journey. Through signs, visions, dreams, and little miracles, they will always show you the way.

26 THE GOLDEN RULE

"I hate that man with every core of my being," the woman shouted. "He's brought nothing but pain and suffering into this world. I wish someone would just put him out of his misery."

The wise old woman responded, "But then… how would he ever learn?" "Learn what? He's as stubborn as they come. That man's not going to learn anything." "Don't be sure. He may be learning a great deal in his final moments. For he's surely not a happy man." The woman shook her head in disagreement, "You know what they say about old dog's learning new tricks. What do you think he could possibly learn at this age?"

The wise woman responded, "Imagine if the man passed to the spirit world today. During his life review he would see all of the mistakes that he made and all of the lessons that he missed. And then eventually he would reincarnate back unto this Earth, having to start from birth all over again." "Maybe that would be for the best. Maybe he could use a fresh start." "Yes, but now is the time for him to learn. For his difficult lessons are at hand. He knows why he is suffering. He knows the mistakes that he has made. This is his opportunity to learn. In this lifetime, not the next."

"Better to let him suffer his lessons now, you're saying, then to start again?" "Exactly, my dear. So, don't pray for the man's demise. For you are simply praying for him to start again. Instead, pray that God will show him the truth of his actions. And pray, that he will learn from his mistakes."

Through an infinity of time, our soul has reincarnated into every existence and every state of being that has ever been.

We are all an extension of God (source), an individual spark of light, each with our own unique personality. In this way, and many others, we are all connected.

As an extension of source, we have experienced, and will experience, every conciseness that has ever existed. Put more simply, at some point, I was you, and you were me.

Consider then how you would apply this spiritual knowledge to your life. Think about that one person that has caused you so much pain. Now consider that at some point, maybe a billion reincarnations ago, you where that very person. You made the same bad choices. You had the same horrible attitude. "There is no way," you might respond. "This person is nothing like me." You're right of course, but this is only because your soul has evolved over many incarnations.

This is why we must embrace the philosophy that is at the core of every major religion, to treat others as you would have them treat you. For in the end, at some point during our soul's existence and evolution, you were them, and they were you.

Live each day with loving intent and a peaceful heart.

In the end, there is only one lesson that matters. Only one commandment that we all must follow.

THE GOLDEN RULE

Christianity: In everything, do to others as you would have them do to you, for this is the law and the profits. – Jesus, Mathew 7:12

Sikhism: I am a stranger to no one, and no one is a stranger to me. Indeed, I am a friend to all. - Guru Granth Sahib, p. 1299

Islam: Not one of you truly believes until you wish for others what you wish for yourself. – The Prophet Muhammad, Hadith

Zoroastrianism: Do not do unto others whatever is injurious to yourself. Shayast-na-Shayast 13.29

Hinduism: This is the sum of duty: do not do to others what would cause pain if done to you. – Mahabharata 5:1517

Buddhism: Treat not others in the ways that you yourself would find hurtful. – Udana-Varga 5.18

27 The Acceptance of Death

A loving wife brought her husband his nightly dinner. He had been bed ridden for a year. As they sat together sharing their meal, he told her of the pain that he was suffering and his inability to sleep at night. "I wish I would die," he said in tears. "I can't take this pain anymore." The wife visibly upset, slammed down her cup. "Don't you ever say that to me again! Do you understand? Don't you ever talk about dying on me again!"

Several months later the man was rushed to the hospital where he suffered his third heart attack. After an hour of work, the staff barely resuscitated the man. "Please, no more," he said to his wife. "You have to let me go. I'm begging you, do not let them resuscitate me again." The wife, still resistant to her husband's request, left the hospital room crying.

Later that night, suffering his fourth heart attack, the man finally passed. His wife devastated, screamed at the hospital staff, "Why did you let him die? Why did you take him from me?"

It took many years, but as the woman grew older her opinion of death slowly changed. She realized that it was here on Earth that she had to suffer through her aches and pains. That it was here that she was left to feel the emotions of loss and regret. "I wish I would have just let him go," she thought to herself. "Why should he have suffered on my account? All that he wanted was to be free of his pain. And now all that I want is to be by his side."

28 Our Connection to the Spirit World

Abigale awoke from a nightmare. In her dream she was being pushed into a dark and smokey room that had been destroyed by a fire. As she stared into the darkness, she sensed a ghostly presence hiding just beyond the shadows. "Show yourself," she said in a soft quivering voice. The door to her closet slowly began to close. Terrified and struggling to breath, she said again, "Show yourself."

Her husband awoke from his sleep, "Are you okay? Who were you speaking to?" "I swear we have a ghost in this house. I've never had nightmares like this before." "Was your dream about the girl again?" "I think so. She was trying to show me how she died. Did this house ever have a fire?" "No, it couldn't have. It's new construction." "Anyway, I'm pretty sure that she died in a fire."

This wasn't the first time that Abigale had a nightmare or sensed a spirit in the house. The televisions in different rooms had turned on in the middle of the night. Orbs had been captured on their security cameras, and items had been moved or went missing. But still, her husband did his best to resist the thought that their house was haunted. "It's new construction," he would always say. But Abigale new the truth.

The next day Abigale met with a well-known medium to ask about the girl. "Yes, my dear, I see her." "Small and skinny with dark hair?" "Exactly!" "Why is she haunting this house?" "I don't believe she is. She followed you home." "From where?" "Let me see… How often do you visit your mother?" "It's been about a month since I visited the cemetery." "And when did your dreams begin?" "Oh my God! Do you think she followed me home? But why? What did I do to her?"

"It's not what you did, it's what you can do. You can sense her presence. She's not trying to hurt you. She's trying to get your attention." "Does she want me to do something?" "I don't think so. She just wants you to know that she exists." "So, what do we do?" "We will pray for her. Pray for her to have peace and pray for her to find God's loving light."

For those spirits who have passed, who are lost on this side and afraid to go into the light, we pray for their souls.

If you want to attract a lower vibrational entity into your life, focus your emotions on fear and anger. If you want to ward off such entities, focus your emotions on the higher vibration of love. For the closer we are to love, the closer we are to God's great light, and the more protected we become.

The same rule applies to the non-spirit world. If you want to draw in the wrong type of people into your life, those who carry a destructive force, focus your attention on the emotions of fear and anger. If you want to find your soulmate, or a supportive friend, focus your emotions on love and appreciation. Light attracts light. Love attracts love.

29 Go Into the Light

A woman died over a hundred years ago. She was shot dead in a brothel alongside her daughter by a jealous customer. Her soul has wondered the same building ever since. "There's no place for me in Heaven," she said to herself. "Only punishments for my sins."

One day, as the spirit looked down upon the hotel lobby, she noticed a peculiar woman checking into her room. There was something special about her. Something about her aura and the way she carried herself. The woman hesitated as she entered her room. She could sense the spirit looking down from above. She quickly turned and looked up into the rafters. The spirit startled, disappeared back into the shadows. "She saw me! How is that possible? Who is this strange woman?"

Later that evening, the spirit noticed a group of people sitting around a large table in one of hotel's dining rooms. They were all holding hands and repeating the same prayer. As the spirit approached, she noticed the same woman looking up at her with a smile. "It's okay. You're welcome here."

The woman then closed her eyes and continued to pray. As she did, other spirits began to enter the room. Some appeared from the shadows, while others appeared from a bright light above. These spirits she could tell, the ones from the light, they were different. They had come to visit their loved ones. They were there to share some important message.

Over the next several hours the spirits of the light took turns speaking through the medium. Once their message was shared, the spirits would fade back into the light. One by one they went, until the light was no more. Until all that remained were the spirits of dark.

"We all must be damned," the spirit thought to herself. "No!" the woman said loudly. "You are not. And if you choose, you can also return to God's loving light." The spirit surprised by the woman's response, backed into the darkness. "Do not be afraid. There's a place for you in Heaven." The sprit backed further away. The woman yelled out, "Your daughter… she is waiting for you there. Salvation, my dear… it's waiting for."

After a long moment of silence, the spirit moved out of the shadows and closer to the woman. "Are you ready to go to her?" the woman asked. "The spirit moved closer to the table. "Let us pray. Dear God, shine your bright light around this lost soul. Show her the way back into your loving arms."

Right at that moment a bright light appeared from above the ceiling. The spirit had seen this light before. It was the light that had called to her when she died. Called her away from this world and away from her daughter. The spirit scared, began to fade away, but then suddenly she heard a soft voice say, "Mamma, it's me. It's your daughter. Come to me Mamma."

We don't have to die to receive the bliss of God's bright light. Regardless of our actions, there is no reason to fear judgement on the other side. Only love and understanding await.

30 A Message from the Spirit World

A grieving daughter visits a medium in an attempt to connect with her mother who had just passed. "We had a pretty rocky relationship," the girl said to the medium. "And with her passing so quickly, I never had a chance to say goodbye." The medium replied with a warm smile, "You know your mother loves you. You don't need me to tell you that." "I know, but it would really help me to heal if I could say I'm sorry. Sorry for all of the stupid fighting. Sorry for being such a difficult child." The medium holding the girl's hand, "Okay honey, let's try to reach her."

After a moment of prayer and silence, the medium said in a soft voice, "Your mother is with us now. She loves you very much and wants you to know that there is nothing to feel sorry about. She wants you to feel at peace about your relationship, and she says that she'll always be with you." As the daughter cried in relief, "Please ask her if there is anything that she has learned from the spirit world that would help me in my life." "Yes, your mother said, there are some things that she wants you to know."

"She wants you to start to enjoy your life. She wants you to smile and laugh, to be silly with your kids... To have fun. She wants you to stop being so serious all the time. She says that she regrets not treating her life as a celebration and that she doesn't want you to make the same mistake."

"She wants you to get in the habit of saying yes. Yes, you will go to the park with your kids. Yes, you will spend time together with your friends. Yes, you will take that class. We are put on this Earth to experience life. So, start experiencing. Start trying new things. Get in the habit of always saying yes."

"She wants you to stop judging others. She wants you to know that we are all connected. We are all one. And that we are all viewed equally in God's eyes. So do your best to treat others with love and understanding and stop holding on to so much anger and hatred in your heart."

"And finally, she wants you to stop worrying about what others think of you. It doesn't matter. Not one bit. She wants you to know that you are perfect just the way you are. And that you should never be afraid to express yourself." The medium pointed at the girl while looking up in the air, "Your mother is saying, always stay true to who you are."

The medium looked back down at the girl and smiled, "That's it. She's left us now." The daughter smiled with tears running down her face, "That was really helpful, thank you." "I'm happy to help. And remember, you can speak to your mother at any time. She is always with you, and she can always hear you."

Celebrate this life. Participate in all of its glory. Stay true to yourself and never worry about the opinions of others.

31 A Past Life Remembered

On the way home from kindergarten, Jasmine asked her mother the oddest question, "When am I going to see my other mommy?" "What are you talking about, honey, I'm your only mommy." "You're my new mommy. I want to see, Julie, my other mother, the one with the brown hair." "Julie!? We don't know a Julie, baby. Do you mean, Grandma June?" "No, Julie. My mommy from the city. The one I lived with before the fire."

Later that evening, the mother asked her daughter about the lady from the city. Jasmine told her that they lived in a townhouse in Chicago. That her previous mother was tall and had a beautiful smile. And apparently they lived in the 70's because Jasmine knew every detail about the bicentennial and the parade that they attended that day.

After gathering a lengthy list of facts, the mother started to investigate online. It wasn't long before she found a newspaper article about Julie Brown and her little boy Tarrence. They had both died in a fire in Chicago in 1975. As she read the article, the mother couldn't believe her eyes. Jasmine had recalled every single fact from the article and several more that she couldn't have known. "How is the possible," she said to herself. "How could she remember her previous life?"

Through years of therapy and past life regression, Jasmine was able to work through her trauma and her great fear of fires. As she did, the memories of her past life slowly started to fade.

When possible, it is always better to deal with our trauma in this life, then to carry it to the next.

32 THE GRAND ASCENSION

Mother Gia, the Earth, has watched as four advanced civilizations have come and gone. The first civilization, the Phaeton's, were destroyed in a great fire. The second race, the Atlanteans, were destroyed by their aggressive pursuit of technology and dangerous experiments with dark matter. No one knows the reason for the demise of the Lemurians, but many suspect it was from a great flood that was triggered by a polar shift. The last race before humankind, the Boeri, fled the Earth due to a nuclear catastrophe. Glass, left behind from the nuclear strike, can still be found in the Peruvian desert.

For those souls who are ready to ascend, the Earth will provide a new home. For others, the opportunity for growth will lay upon another planet.

Too much time has been wasted for another civilization to fail once again. And therefore, it has been decided by our creators and those who watch upon us, that it is time for this planet to ascend to a higher dimensional plane. This new planet, new Earth, will be occupied by those souls who are ready to elevate their state of consciousness. To move away from such lower vibrational energies found in fear, anger and greed, and toward higher energies found in peaceful enlightenment and love.

And so, a choice must be made by us all to be shown through our actions and intentions. Will we remain a lower vibrational being trapped in this never-ending wheel of karma? Or will we ascend toward the light, to join our cosmic brethren?

33 Heaven and Hell on Earth

A son sat next to his mother on the subway train home. Across from them was a homeless man, passed out and asleep. A crowd of people came and went as the train stopped at each station, but the homeless man never moved. "How could he sleep like that?" the boy asked his mother. Shaking her head she replied, "Try not to stare."

As the train approached its final stop, the man slid down from his seat and laid lifeless on the subway floor. "Oh my God!" a lady shouted out. "Somebody should call an ambulance. He's not breathing." But as soon as the train doors opened, the man was quickly forgot. Not a single person called for help. No one stayed behind. The man just laid there as the crowd went on their way.

"What's going to happen to that man?" the boy asked his mother as they rushed down the stairs. "Who knows?" the mother replied. "Come on, we have to go. We're going to be late." "Well, what happens when we die?" "You mean physically or spiritually?" "Well both… I guess. What will happen to the man?" "Well, I assume the city will bury his body if they can't find his relatives." "And spiritually?" "I guess he will either go to heaven or hell depending upon if he was a good or bad."

As they continued to walk down the busy sidewalk the boy looked up at the lights of the city. "If this isn't heaven and hell then I don't know what is." "What?" The mother startled by her son's statement stopped to ask, "What do you mean by that?"

The boy continued, "That man, he died alone. He was homeless and hungry and not a single person cared. No one even stopped to help. If this isn't hell, then I don't what is." The mother responded in a concerned voice, "I'm sorry that you had to see that, but things aren't usually this bad."

"I know," the boy said as he looked up. "Look at all of the beauty around us. It's heaven here as well." "I guess you're right... I shouldn't have said that the man could go to hell. I'm sure he went to heaven."

The mother held her son's hand tightly as they continued down the sidewalk. The boy smiled and said, "I think he just went somewhere to rest. Some place that he could sleep in peace." "I'm sure you're right." "He'll come back when he wakes up. Back to give it another try."

Do not fear going to hell, for if you choose, it is all around you.

Do not ponder on the hopes of going to heaven, for it is already here within your reach.

34 The Correct Path is Not Always Clear

For two days the pirate ship continued its aggressive pursuit. The captain, concerned for the life of his crew began to pray, "Dear God, protect the lives of these good men and women. Our is a path is righteous. Our mission, to bring culture and knowledge to these indigenous people, a blessed one."

A few hours later the ship was captured and boarded. Life was lost, and most of the bounty in the form of food, seed, and supplies were taken. The remaining crew, along with their captain, were forced to return home back to Spain.

Upon his return, the captain was forced to face the high court. "I know that I failed you, but if given another chance, I swear on my life that we will complete this mission." "Did you not hear?" a member of the court replied. "The men that stole your bounty, they're all dead." "Dead? Did the guard capture them?" "No, apparently the blankets on your ship were carrying the dreaded measles disease." "I don't understand?" "It's a blessing that no one on your ship got sick and fortunate that you never reached the mainland." The captain speaking softly to himself, "We would have killed them all. I was caring nothing but death and destruction and I didn't even know it."

Be flexible in your journey. What may seem like your destiny, may actually be your demise.

We are all taught to put our heads down and to work tirelessly toward our goals and ambitions, but never fear or resist change. Flow like water though the path of life. Be flexible, be aware, and understand that you are being guided each step of the way.

35 Intentions Matter

A woman standing in line with a full cart of groceries noticed the man behind her holding a few items in his hand. Even though she was in a rush, she kindly asked if the man would like to go ahead of her in line. After the man checked out, he handed the cashier $40 to help pay for the woman's groceries. He thanked the woman for her kindness letting her know that he was running late for an extremely important appointment.

We act in kindness and with love, not for some reward awaiting us in this life or the next, but for the joy and fulfillment that the act itself gives us in this very moment.

The positive karma from the woman's kind action was not in the $40 received. This was the proverbial "icing on the cake." The karma received was in the pleasant feeling (vibrational state) that her and the man shared as a result of her kind action.

If the woman would have had the slightest expectation that she might receive some reward for her good deed, monetary or otherwise, then no lesson would have been learned. No karmic debt released. Instead, this would have simply been a friendly transaction shared between two individuals.

Remember the primary lesson found in all religions, "the Golden Rule," treat others in the same manner that you would like to be treated yourself. Put love and kindness out into the world, and it will be returned many-fold.

36 Working with Your Soul Group

"What an eccentric group of characters that we have in our life," Alex said to his sister. "Each one nuttier then the next." "Yeah, but you know that you love them all." "I guess, but I don't understand why God put me with these people. I mean, couldn't we have had just a normal family like everyone else?"

"Maybe," she replied, "or maybe they're all just perfect in their own way." "Ha! Perfect? In what way?" "You're probably the most independent person that I've ever met." "Yeah, that's a good thing." "Imagine if you'd grown up in a strict household." "I don't think I could have made it." "Exactly!" "But Mom and Dad tolerated all of the sneaking out. Being gone for days. Basically, doing whatever you wanted to do. Do you think any other parents would have put up with that?" "You have a point. They were pretty tolerant of my behavior."

"And what about our uncles?" "Exactly my point! They're all crazier than hell." "Yeah but, think about how much time they spent with you when you were younger. They taught you how to fish, how to hunt, and they took you camping all the time. They may all seem crazy now but they all helped to raise us."

Alex, persistent in his argument, "What about Grandpa Tom? I don't think there's anything positive that you can say about him. He brought nothing put pain and suffering to the family." "Yeah, he's a tough one all right. I don't have a ton of good things to say about him either, except that I'm appreciative for all of the things he taught us." "What do you mean? How not to act? How not to treat people? How not to be abusive and demanding? Is that what he taught us?" "That's exactly what he taught us. Look at you. You're an excellent father. One of the most loving men that I've ever known. You didn't learn that from our parents." "Well, I sure as hell didn't learn it from grandpa." "Don't be so sure. I can recall you saying many times that you didn't want to be anything like him when you grew up. Well guess what, you're not."

"Anyway, it's always the kids that grow up in the "normal families" that seem to have the most problems. Is it because their lives are too easy? Maybe growing up in a "crazy" family is what helps you to stay normal?"

We choose our supporting cast of characters. Each with a specific role to play. Each with an important purpose.

Before we reincarnate into this life, we choose our soul group and the roles that we will play. We switch from husband to wife, from parent to child, from friend to adversary. We do this with the purpose to learn from each other. To act as both teacher and student. So that we can each complete our soul's contract.

So, the next time you see that crazy uncle or difficult parent, ask yourself, what role were they meant to play? What lessons were they meant to teach? How can I best serve them, as they have surely served me?"

37 Karma and Intentions

A dirty politician contacted his friend at the IRS. "You have to launch a criminal investigation into Smith's campaign. They're stealing money left and right." "You're wanting to submit a criminal complaint against your biggest political rival?" "No... I want you to submit a complaint against Smith. This way you'll get the credit. You'll be the hero." The IRS agent pondered his response, "But we have no evidence... No one has filed a single complaint." "Come on, you know this guy is dirty. Have you seen his house, the car he drives? How do you think he affords to take his family on all of those extravagant trips?" "Well, he does live a luxurious lifestyle, that's for sure." The politician shook the IRS agent's hand. "This is going to be a big step for your career. Don't forget who pointed you in the right direction when you take over the department."

The truth of the matter was that the politician had no idea if Smith was dirty or not. But he justified his actions by telling himself, "Everyone in politics is corrupt. It's just a matter of who is smart and who gets caught."

A few weeks later the IRS agent launched a criminal investigation into Smith's political campaign. His justification, "his lavish lifestyle." The investigation went on for several years, but no substantial evidence was ever found. In many ways the investigation ended up helping Smith and his campaign. It showed to his constituents that he ran a tight ship. It showed that not everyone who is in politics or who is successful is corrupt.

As fate would have it, several years later Smith was approached by a large donor who was upset with his rival's campaign. The donor, through a large super pack, had contributed over $100,000. Shortly after this donation was made, the politician paid a high-profile attorney this exact amount to fight off a serious accusation of an ethics violation.

Smith was a shrewd politician. He knew that shouting accusations to the press or filing a complaint with the political watchdog groups would have little effect. So instead, he decided to right a simple letter of inquiry to the IRS's criminal division seeking guidance for his own campaign.

"To ensure that I'm fully compliant with use of political campaign funds received from a super-pack, I am requesting the following guidance… As an example, a donor recently shared with me his concern that congressman Jones used $100,000, which was funneled through a super-pack, to pay for his personal legal fees. My campaign's compliance department and legal team is struggling to find the regulations that support this practice…."

Soon after, the dirty politician was indicted by the IRS for stealing campaign funds. As you would expect, the $100,000 used to pay for his legal fees was just the tip of the iceberg.

Karma will always be repaid, which is why, crime never pays.

No need to wish purely upon your enemies. For karma will always be served to those who are in need. Instead, always pray for the truth to be revealed and for their lessons to be learned.

38 Know What Is at Risk

The young mountain climber pulled his body over the edge of the rocky tower. Catching his breath, he stared out at the lush evergreen valley below. "I did it!" he said to himself as a huge sense of relief rushed through his body. "I can't believe I did it."

After a moment of rest, the climber started to consider the best path down. He didn't have enough rope to repel down the tower so, climbing down the steep face seemed like his only option. But then, he noticed a large flat shelf sticking out from the other side. "If I can make it to that shelf, then it's an easy climb down." As he stared at the rocky bottom far below, "But, if I don't make it, I'm going to break my neck."

The climber spent the next 20 minutes staring at the shelf across and the deep crevasse below. "Come on, you can do it!" he said to himself. "One easy jump and you're home free." After finally mustering up the courage, the climber threw his gear across the five-foot gap. Then after several deep breaths he said to himself in a nervous voice, "One, two, three, GO!" The young man sprinted across the tower surface and jumped high into the air. His body reaching the other side, slide across the flat shelf and slammed into the back of the rocky wall. "Oh, my God!" he said to himself. "That was scary. I'll never do that again."

With his adrenaline running high, the climber made his way down the rocky trail to the bottom of the mountain where his mentor, a much older and more seasoned climber, was waiting. "Why did you take such stupid risk?" the mentor asked. "What do you mean?" "You saw it, I made that jump easy." "Yeah, but at what risk?" "Isn't that the whole point of why we climb? For the exhilaration? To feel alive?"

"No, not at all," the mentor replied. "For the challenge, for the accomplishment, yes. For a stupid risk just to get a temporary rush, no, never." The mentor continued as the young climber dropped his gear in frustration. "The thing is, I don't think you even know what you're risking." "I know what I'm risking. Some broken bones... maybe my life. But I'm okay with that." Shaking his head, the mentor continued, "No, you're not just risking your life. You're risking your children's life and their children's life." "What children?" "The children that you'll never have because you died jumping over that steep crack."

He continued, "You're risking so much more than know. You're risking all of the wonderful experiences that you're still yet to have. All of the places that you'll one day visit. The beautiful people that you'll meet..." "Okay, okay, I get it. I guess it's not just about me wanting to feel brave." The mentor laughed as he hugged the young man, "You just climbed to the top of a 200-foot rock tower by yourself. Trust me, you're brave. Now, be brave and smart, okay?" The young climber responded with a smile on his face, "You're right. I'll be smarter next time."

Your soul chose to reincarnate unto this Earth, one of the most challenging schools in the Universe, you are brave. Now be brave and smart and take great care of this precious life.

39 THE BRAVEST OF SOULS

Sabbatian is a lovely child who was born with a severe case of autism. Even though it has been challenging at times, his parents love him desperately and are so appreciative that he is in their life. A foolish relative once asked, "Don't you wish there was a magic pill that could just heal his afflictions and make him like everyone else?" His mother patiently responded, "For him I do. You always want the best for your children and you never want to see them suffer. But for me, I'm just grateful to have Sabbatian in my life. He has taught me so much." "Really? Like what?" "He's taught me about compassion, and what true love is… I used to think I knew what love was, but I never understood what true unconditional love was until I met my son. He has taught the true meaning of love. About kindness. About compassion… and so much more."

Bravest is the soul who chooses to come to this Earth to teach us through their afflictions.

Every challenge that we face in this life, every burden, every affliction, especially those related to our health, is carefully chosen by our higher souls before we reincarnate unto this Earth. The greater the affliction, the more Karma released, and the more spiritual growth incurred.

Brave is the sole who chooses to come to this Earth, and even braver, the soul who agrees to teach others through their physical afflictions. This is why it is often said that there are more souls waiting in Heaven for children with disabilities than there are for those who are healthy.

40 The Law of Connections

A son said to his father, "It doesn't matter, you made bad grades when you were young and you're doing well." "It doesn't matter?" the father responded. "Trust me, every choice you make, they're all connected, they all matter." "What does that mean?" "It means if you slack off in your homework today, you will be forming a new habit. A habit which will eventually affect the grades in all of your classes. This habit may end up limiting what colleges you attend. What career choices you have…" The son putting his books back on the table, "Okay, okay, I get it."

The father continued, "It's really true, and these connections become so apparent the older you get. Even trivial things like your health. I ask myself, "Is the ringing in my ears from listening to loud music when I was a kid? How could I have been so stupid? Am I going to need a hearing aid now?" Trust me, every bad choice you make will follow you into the future, but every good choice will reward you and build upon the next."

"Do your homework, don't do your homework, in the end, it's up to you. You can take always take the easy path. But eventually if you want to perform in school, you'll need to correct course. And the farther you are down a given path, the harder it will be to adjust."

Brick by brick, lesson by lesson, each decision effecting the next. Our choices all connected, our past and future, all represented in this very moment.

Mastering the Mind

Lead with confidence, intelligence, and strategy, and never with blind emotions.

I am a powerful being and I am in control of what I manifest I am happy. I am strong. I am protected and I am loved. And I am so very appreciative for this life that I have been given.

I am so very grateful for all of the hidden blessings that this challenge has provided.

An item can always be replaced, but time and happiness are irreplaceable. So, don't waste it worrying about the little things

Self-perfection starts with a journey of self-love.

A victory won out of anger is always fleeting. The loss incurred from our poor actions, often permanent.

Fear will always cripple your senses and blind your good reason.

The only embarrassment in life is the refusal to try.

You hold the key to your own cage, and the key is fear.

All of the wisdom that we have learned, not meant to be left behind on the battlefield. Teach them how you have survived. Put down your sword and share your vast knowledge.

Our emotions are our beacon, always drawing closer that which we feel. So, be mindful of your emotions so that you don't manifest that which you fear.

Never worry about the winding path, with patience and persistency, God will always show you the way.

No need for a crystal ball, in the end, everything will be okay.

To have faith is not to be blind to the obstacles ahead, but to know that there's always light at the end of each tunnel.

I'm happy in this moment so my life is grand. I'm sad in the next, so it's all gone to hell. Our emotions ever fleeting, our perception of our reality, always changing.

Thoughts lead to feelings, feelings to vibrations, vibrations to manifestation. So, always be mindful of your thoughts. For your thoughts can often cancel out your prayers.

It's impossible to manifest something positive when your focused on the negatives. It's impossible to move forward when your focused on the past.

To heal we must put aside our anger, our desire to be right, and focus on the things that we appreciate.

41 Lead with Strategy Not Emotions

A huge sonic boom shook the submarine knocking most of the crew to the ground. "Captain, we've taken on major damage. We have to surface before our engine fails." "We'll be sitting ducks," the second in command shouted. The captain calmly responded, "Slow to surface." "Are you crazy?" said the second in command. "Their battleship will fire upon us the moment we surface." The captain spoke to the helmsman, "Nice and slow." "Aye, captain." The submarine's sail slowly crested from beneath the water's surface. "Bearing set at one-five-zero. Maintaining speed at zero six knots." "Hold your course."

The captain looking through the telescope, spotted a large battleship heading in their direction. After a moment of silent contemplation, he grabbed the ship's microphone and addressed the crew. "This is your captain speaking. As you know, the ship has taken on great damage. Our back two quarters are flooded and our engine is starting to fail. If we submerse, we are likely to sink. But now that we've surfaced, we're exposed to our enemy."

The captain looked at his crew, "I am proud of you all. Your sacrifice and bravery will be celebrated by your countrymen." After standing for a moment in silence he continued, "However... I'm not ready to surrender quite yet." The men on the ship begin to cheer. "There's only one ship on the surface and one submarine below. We have faced much greater odds and have always survived. And so, as we've done many times before, we will use our strategy and wit to survive another day."

As the men continued to cheer, the second in command addressed the captain in a quiet voice. "What is our plan captain? Do you intend to surrender?" "Surender!? Who spoke of surrendering? Are the torpedoes fully loaded and counter measures set?" "Yes, captain, should we fire while we still have the advantage?" "No, we will maintain a slow and steady course headed towards the homeland." "Your plan is to run away?" "No, the battle has already been lost. We know it, and they know it. But they also know, if they attempt to sink us, we will have no option but to respond."

"So, you're proposing a truce? And you think they will honor this request?" The captain calmly responded, "I'm giving our enemy the benefit of the doubt." "That they will show mercy on us?" "No, not at all. I'm assuming, that their captain will put strategy over emotion." "I don't understand?" "It's a simple question. Would it be worth the cost of a healthy battleship to take down a crippled submarine?" The second in command sat in silence as he considered the question. "No, I guess not, captain." "We will wisely retreat for now, so that we can live to fight another day." "Aye, captain, aye."

Lead with confidence, intelligence, and strategy, and never with blind emotions.

42 The Power of "I Am"

Renee was walking in the park thinking about a demanding situation in her life. She found herself repeating the same words over and over. "I want..." "I want to be done with this. I want to move on. I want a better life..."

Her angels seeing her intent to manifest desire spoke to her and said, "Yes, my child, we do see your intention to hold desire in your heart." Confused and upset Renee responded, "My intention is not to manifest desire. It's to manifest change." "Then why are you telling us what you want? To manifest change, you must tell us what you are."

It was hard, and it took a conscious effort, but from that moment forward Renee forced herself to replace the words "I want" with "I am." "I am free of matter. I have put this behind me now. I am proud of myself for learning this lesson. I am strong. I am resilient. I am free of this now."

The moment that Renee started to use the words, "I am" instead of "I want," was the exact moment that she freed herself emotionally from this troubling event. Everything else related to this challenge was just small insignificant details to be worked out at a later time and place. Realizing this victory, she said to herself. "I am free. I am free. Dear God, thank you for letting me know that I am free."

I am a powerful being and I am in control of what I manifest. I am happy. I am strong. I am protected and I am loved. And I am so very appreciative for this life that I have been given.

43 THE POWER OF APPRECIATION

I was dealing with a stressful situation in my life that seemed to never end. In an effort to cope, I would spend every morning thinking about the matter during my morning walk and then I would put it set it aside for the rest of the day. Although these walks were therapeutic, I realized that I wasn't truly healing from my pain. I needed to find a way to heal, to find peace, and to put this matter behind me once for all.

The next day, as I started my walk I thought, "That would have never occurred if it wasn't for this event." Number two, "I surely would have had to deal with this other thing if this didn't happen first." Number three, "Now, once this this is over, I'll have this new positive thing in my life..." By the end of my one-hour walk I had completed a mental list of over 100 things for which I was grateful. These were not things like, "I'm happy to have good health." This was a list that was specific to this very challenge. After reflecting on this extensive list, I then asked myself, "With so many unintentional blessings that have occurred from this one "bad" event, how can I possibly be upset that this happened?"

I am so very grateful for all of the hidden blessings that this challenge has provided.

Of all the tools that we have in your arsenal to deal with the endless challenges in our life, by far the most remarkable is the power of appreciation. So be grateful for every lesson and pay attention to its many hidden blessings.

44 Don't Sweat the Small Stuff

A grandson enjoyed a cold glass of tea with his beloved grandfather. "Grandpa, what's the best part of growing old?" After a moment of reflection he responded, "The best part of growing old is that you stop sweating the small stuff." "You mean, you stop caring?" "No, you still care but the little things don't bother you as much. Good things happen, bad things happen, whatever it is you learn to just roll with the punches."

The grandfather continued, "Remember how upset you were when you lost your bicycle?" "Yeah! I'm still upset." "Now imagine over your lifetime you had bikes stolen, cars stolen, horses went missing… By the time you've reached my age, you've lost about every type of transportation that you've ever owned. The grandson stood up in amazement, "You've had your car stolen?" "Sure, a couple of times, but I always got a new one." "They took your car and you didn't get upset?" "Heavens no. I got really upset. The first time it happened I spent months driving around town looking for the culprits. Believe me, I was about as mad as you could be. But in the end, the car was gone, and that was that.

The grandson still in shock, "And then it happened again?" Yes, but I had learned my lesson. I could've gotten angry again. I could've wasted my time searching for the car and the criminals. But instead, I decided to just get on with it. I figured, they already stole my car, why the hell would I also give them my happiness?"

"So, what would you do if someone stole your car today? Laughing, the grandfather replied, "That piece of junk? I'd send them a thank you letter." "So, you wouldn't even care?" "Sure, I'd care, but it would not bother me that much." The grandfather leaned in as if to tell some grand secret. "Some things will break. Some will be lost. And some even stolen. But remember, only you can give away your happiness. So, don't sweat the small stuff."

The grandson sat back in his chair and contemplated his grandfather's advice. "You know what else I've learned?" the grandfather asked. "What's that?" "The stuff you lose. It always gets replaced. And most of the time with better stuff. Just like your bicycle. Before you know it, you will have a new bike. Nicer than the one you had before. And then you'll wonder, "Was it really worth getting so upset?"

An item can always be replaced, but time and happiness are irreplaceable. So, don't waste it worrying about the little things.

45 Be in the Moment

A castaway sat silent on the beach staring out into the south Pacific Ocean. His plane had crashed several weeks ago, and it was only by chance that he came upon this small tropical island.

After gathering enough food and water for the day, the man sat down at the same spot and looked out into the ocean. He missed the company of his wife. He worried about his children. He replayed all of the mistakes of his life in his head. He wished he could do things differently. If only given one more chance...

Six months later, a fishing boat with two men found the man's body lying near the shore. "How do you think he died?" one asked. "I don't know. This island has a lagoon so, there is plenty of fresh water. There's pineapple and coconut trees everywhere, so he couldn't have starved." Examining his body more closely, "Yeah, it's weird. It's as if he just sat down and decided to die."

"Do not dwell in the past, do not dream of the future, concentrate the mind on the present moment." - Buddha

We all too often, spend our days full of regret thinking about the past and our nights worrying about the future. Instead, we should embrace this very moment and all that it has to offer. For the future may never come and the past is long behind us.

46 Can't Hate Ourselves Into Change

If you ever wanted to hear a gloomy perspective of the world, Mark would be the first one to call. But for all of his criticism, the person that Mark is the hardest on is himself. The funny thing is, if you ask him why he's so negative, he'll tell you that he's not negative at all. Instead, he would say that he was just a perfectionist, and that we should all hold ourselves to the same ambitious standards.

Self-perfection starts with a journey of self-love.

The challenge with Mark's philosophy, is that we can't hate ourselves into becoming a better person. Even with the best intentions, having the mindset that you're constantly failing only manifests more failure.

Imagine a little league baseball player stepping up to bat with the internal dialog, "I really suck at this game. This pitcher is so fast, there is no way I'm going to hit the ball..." These are not the words of a perfectionist. They're the words of someone who is manifesting failure.

"I am getting better every day. I will hit the ball. I'm having fun regardless of the outcome." These are the words of a self-loving soul who is manifesting perfection.

47 The Damage Caused by Anger

There wasn't a conversation that would pass when Karen wouldn't play the victim. It was if she got up every day looking for a fight and someone to blame. Anger wasn't just a fleeting emotion. It was the energy she needed to get through the day. It didn't matter if she was right or wrong, victory, the feeling of domination over another, this was her most powerful aphrodisiac.

Driving home she noticed a young man following a little too close in his car. As she stared at him through the rearview mirror, she saw the man glance down at his phone. This of course made Karen furious. When the light turned green, she started to roll forward and then slammed on her brakes. The young man startled, also slammed on his breaks stopping just inches from Karen's car. "I knew it!" she screamed. "I'm calling the police."

Karen spent the next 20 minutes yelling at the man before the police finally arrived. "There he is officer. He was following me for miles, harassing me, trying to slam into my car. I'm surprised he didn't flee the scene." The woman storming over to the young man pointing her finger, "That's him, arrest him."

The young man had spent the last 20 minutes sitting in silence. So, many times he wanted to respond to Karen's wild accusations but he knew that it would only make things worse. She had kicked his car. Spit on his windshield. Called him every name of the book. But he just sat there in calm silence waiting patiently for the police to arrive.

"Well, son, were you harassing this lady?" the officer asked. "No, sir, I have the whole thing recorded on my dash camara. As you will see I was not following this lady at all. And it's clear that she slammed on the breaks so that I would hit her."

As the officers watched the video Karen yelled out, "What?! Did he tell you a bunch of lies? That video doesn't prove anything!" The police officers pulled out their handcuffs and placed them around Karen's wrist. "Are you serious? You're taking his side? He hit me, you idiot."

A victory won out of anger is always fleeting. The loss incurred from our poor actions, often permanent.

There are a certain set of emotions that can destroy our lives and anger is one of them. It is a destructive force that is in direct opposition to the vibrational state of love. Never decide or act out of anger. The victory will be fleeting and the loss will often be permanent.

48 The Damage Caused by Fear

As Karen sat in the police station holding tank, she became overwhelmed with a sense of fear. "These bastards are going to lock me up for a crime that I didn't even commit." Her breath becoming shorter and shorter, "I've heard about stories like this. I'm never going to get out of here." As she embraced her fear, her body slowly became crippled with stress and anxiety.

By the time Karen appeared in front of the judge the next day she was a basket case. Her attorney repeated to her, "For the last time, all you need to do is to apologize for your behavior and promise to take it easy." "You just want me to admit I'm guilty." "No," the attorney shouted back. "Can't you see I'm trying to keep you out of jail?" "Do you think I trust you? You're just as bad as they are!"

The judge sentenced Karen to 30 days in jail for making false allegations against the young man. During her time in prison, she learned many painful lessons. She learned how it felt to be dominated by others. To have anger thrust upon her. But she also learned many positive lessons as well. She learned about sympathy and compassion. She learned how destructive emotions of anger and fear had destroyed her life. She learned about the person that she had been and the person that she now inspired to be.

Fear will always cripple your senses and blind your good reason.

49 Never Be Embarrassed

I couldn't figure it out. For the fourth year in a row, my son was not playing any sports teams. It made no sense. He was in great physical shape and all of his friends played at least on one team. I asked him, "Why aren't you going out for any sports this year?" He replied, "Remember a few years ago when I tried to play baseball?" "Yeah, that coach was a nightmare." "I was so embarrassed. I had no idea what I was doing. I never want to go through that again." "Well, I certainly won't make you play, but please keep a few things in mind before you make your decision."

"The first, is that you should never, ever, care about what other people think about you. What someone thinks about someone else, has nothing to do with that person and everything to do with how they think of themselves. Remember most people, especially your friends, want you to succeed. If they're laughing, it's to tell you it's okay, that it's no big deal."

"Also, making mistakes is one of the best ways to lean. Instead of being embarrassed, you should embrace your mistakes. Take joy in them. There's no sin in screwing up, only in making the same mistake over and over again."

The only embarrassment in life is the refusal to try.

Our greatest self-inflicted sin is our refusal to try. To hide behind our shame and embarrassment. To surrender to our fears. Don't let them steal one precious moment from your life. Don't give away a single cherished experience.

50 The Nothing to Fear But Fear Itself

As a mother comforted her teenage daughter, "What's wrong?" "Tony," her boyfriend for the past two years, "he's cheating on me!" "What makes you say that?" "I just know it. I can tell by the way he's acting." The mother gently rubbed her daughter's back, "So, what?" "So, what! So, if he is, I'll die!"

"You know that won't happen. What would really happen if he's cheating on you? What would be the big deal?" The daughter confused by her mother's question, "What would be the big deal? I would probably spend the rest of my life alone, or even worse, I'd have to marry some loser like Jerry." "Common, you're a beautiful girl and the world is full of plenty of men who would like to date you." The mother gently asked again, "What would really happen if he cheated on you?"

The daughter starting to catch her breath, "We would break up, that's what." "Sure, then what?" "My heart would be broken." "Indeed, for a while, then what?" The daughter sat in silence contemplating the question as the mother asked again, "Then what?" "I don't know." "Then after time, not even that long, the pain would go away. Then after a little more time, you'd date someone else. Someone a little nicer. Even a little more handsome. Eventually you'd meet the love of your life, and do you know what you'd say then?" "What?!" "Thank God Tony cheated on me! If not, I would've never met this perfect man."

You hold the key to your own cage, and the key is fear.

The next time you find yourself consumed with fear, ask, what would actually happen if this occurred? Of course, it would be horrible and painful, but what would actually happen and what would you do? Would you survive it? Would you eventually move on? In the end, would it make you a better person? The point of the exercise is not to wallow in your fear, but to come to the realization that there's nothing to fear. That no matter how painful the event, eventually everything will be okay.

Remember, thoughts plus emotions, equal manifestations. So be mindful of your emotions. Otherwise, you will unintentionally manifest the very thing that you fear. Instead of focusing on what may happen, focus on the solutions to your problems and the peace ahead once the problem is resolved.

51 Time to Put Down Your Weapons

A great knight returned to his king victorious in his quest. He had slayed the three headed dragon and returned the king's daughter safe and unharmed. "For how do I serve thee, my king?" the knight asked. "What glorious battle lay ahead?" The king smiled, "No, my son, your battles are no more. You have earned your freedom and a place by my side." The knight with mixed emotions, slowly stood. "It is time for you to relinquish your sword. From now on you will wear the parliamentary robe. Your greatest weapon, your judgment and strong wit."

Two young squires approached the knight to receive his shield and armor. In its place, he was handed an elegant blue robe made of soft cotton and imported silk. The king, sensing the knight's dissatisfaction, "Are you not pleased with these gifts?" "I am, my king." "Then why do you cast such sadness upon my court?" "These weapons, they are all that I know. My armor, my second skin. My sword, it's who I am."

The king stood and spoke in a kind voice, "There are times in our life that we must battle, and times that we must rest. Rest your heart, great knight. Rest your resolve. Share with our people the lessons that you have learned from your battles. Show them how you survived. This is how you can best serve me now."

All of the wisdom that we have learned, not meant to be left behind on the battlefield. Teach them how you have survived. Put down your sword and share your vast knowledge.

52 Be Mindful of Your Fear

Two hunters sat on the edge of the jungle in India. One said to the other, "Should we worry about tigers?" The other laughed, "Until now, no. But now that you've given the tiger our attention, maybe so." "What do you mean?!" "Until you give something your attention, it's as if it doesn't exist. Now that we've given the tiger our thoughts, our energy, now it has manifested as part of our reality." "Oh no! What do we do? The last thing that I want to do is to attract a tiger." The hunter put down his gun and calmly sat down. "The first thing you need to do, is to take a deep breath and relax. The more energy you give the tiger, the more likely it is to appear."

As the younger hunter nervously paced back and forth, "It's dangerous out here. Don't you ever worry about getting hurt?" "There's a significant difference between being mindful and being afraid." Encouraging the younger hunter to sit by his side, "Yes, of course I'm aware that we share this jungle with the tiger. After all, this is its home. But to worry, is to give it our attention, our energy. When we do this, we give the tiger an invitation to join us. So yes, be mindful, be aware, but don't be afraid. Remember, the tiger can smell your fear a mile away."

Our emotions are our beacon, always drawing closer that which we feel. So, be mindful of your emotions so that you don't manifest that which you fear.

53 Everything is Fine In this Moment

Deep in the Peruvian jungle an English explorer yelled out to his guide, "We've been on this God forsaken trail for six days now. When are we going to reach the temple?" "Soon," the guide replied. "I don't think you understand, we are running out of food and water." "We have plenty for today, no need to worry." "Well, I do worry you see. That's my job, to keep us all alive." "God will do that. We just need to keep moving forward."

That evening the skies grew dark and it began to rain. Sheets of water cascaded down from the trees flooding the trails. The explorer yelled out, "Now what are we going to do? All of the trails have been washed away. How are we going to survive if we can't even move?" "We will wait," the guide replied. "We have everything we need... food, water, shelter." "You mean, we have everything that we need today?! What about tomorrow? And what about the day after that?" "It does not serve us to worry about such things as they are out of our control. We will wait, we will stay patient, and soon enough the path will appear."

The men sat under their tents in pouring rain for three days while scouts were sent out in every direction. One of them returned exhausted and covered in mud. "We've been heading in the wrong direction. The temple is that way, a few miles over that ridge."

The guide leaning forward with a warm smile, "You see my friend, there was no need to worry. What seemed like our curse," looking up at the rain, "was actually our blessing." As he stretched his legs the guide continued, "The rain, it forced us to sit still, it helped us to gain our bearings. And now that we are rested, the jungle has shown us the way."

Never worry about the winding path, with patience and persistency, God will always show you the way.

Manage with great care and attention the things in this moment that you can control, your thoughts, your emotional wellbeing, your actions towards others. Let your intentions be known to yourself and to your angels, but never suffer needlessly toward a future that you can't control. For there is only one true moment in time, and that moment is now.

54 Live Every Day Like It's Your Last

Lila is a cancer survivor. She has spent the last three years in remission, and with her recent prognosis, is finally hopeful for a full recovery. Her friend, Mindy, cautiously responded to the news, "Don't you worry that the cancer going to come back?" Lila shaking her head, "Worry? No. What's the point? I've already spent too much time worrying. If I've learned anything, it's that life is too short to worry. I'm healthy now. That's all that matters."

Mindy regretting her question, "You're right. I'm just a worry wort. You know that." Lila responded, "So, worry about yourself. I don't need anyone worrying about me." "I do, trust me." "Yeah, I know and you need to stop. Like I said, life's too short." "You're right, I really need to be more positive."

Lila continued, "Imagine if you had a crystal ball that would let you see into the future. You would see some struggles, some difficulties, but in the end, you'd see that everything would work out fine. Now imagine if you knew this, that everything in your life will be fine, but you still chose to worry. Wouldn't that be a waste of life? Wouldn't that be a sin?" "A sin?" "That you were given this precious life and you wasted it, worrying all the time." Mindy, not convinced by her friend's argument, "But that's the problem. We don't have a crystal ball. And we don't know that everything will be okay." "Well, I believe we do, and the news of my recovery is the perfect example."

No need for a crystal ball, in the end, everything will be okay.

55 The Enteral Optimist

The conductor yelled out, "We need more power!" as the train began to slip off the icy rails. "Were not going to make it!" the engineer yelled back. "We'll make it. Just keep shoveling that coal." The train began to shutter as the wheels underneath the locomotive began to spin. "I'm telling you, it's too icy!" "Keep going," the conductor yelled back. "We're going to make it." Just then, a load bang and shutter echoed throughout the train as the wheels began to grip the tracks.

The captain smiled in relief and calmly said to his engineer, "We're going to make it." The engineer wiping his brow, smiled back, "Sorry, boss. As usual, you were right." "No worries. These icy mountains can get a little tricky at times." "Well, Cap, as everyone always says, you are the enteral optimist." "Optimist? Yeah, I guess that's the right word." "What do you mean?" "Some people have what I call blind positivity. No matter what's going on their life, or what obstacle they face, they always have a positive outlook. The optimist, however, recognizes the danger ahead, but chooses to believe that the best outcome will occur. So, yes, you have to be an optimist in order to ride these icy rails." "That's for sure, Captain." As the engineer continued to shovel coal into the fire, "That's for darn sure."

To have faith is not to be blind to the obstacles ahead, but to know that there's always light at the end of each tunnel.

56 BE BRAVE

Sabrina slammed her schoolbooks down on the kitchen counter. "What was I thinking?" "Bad day at school?" her father replied. "I have to give my campaign speech tomorrow in front of the whole school." "You're going to do great. Everyone knows you'd make a fantastic class president." "You don't understand, I've been having panic attacks all day. There's no way that I'm going to get up in front of the school just to look like an idiot." The father hugged his daughter, "I understand. Speaking in public can be terrifying, but no worries, I'll help you to get prepared." "You don't understand. It's not my speech I'm worried about." "I know. I've had to give lots of speeches, and just like you, I was always nervous. But if you give me the chance, I bet I can help."

"The first thing that we need to do is to make sure that you're fully prepared." "What?! I know my speech inside and out." "That's great. But let's also get you prepared to speak in front of an audience. First you can present to me. Then to your mother and your brother. Then we'll record you… The more you practice speaking in front of others, the more confident you'll feel on the stage."

"We can practice all you want," Sabrina responded. "But I'm still going to be scared." "Why? I mean, what's the worst that can happen?" "Every single kid in the school will make fun of me until the day I graduate." "Unlikely, but okay. What's the best thing that can happen?" "I'd give an amazing speech and win the election." "That's right. And how would that feel?" "Great of course, but…" "But what? See there's your problem." "What!?" "It's your mindset. You're setting yourself up for failure. You're thinking about every little thing that could go wrong instead of every little thing that could go right. No wonder why you're terrified." "I know but I can't help it."

"You know what I always tell myself before giving a big speech? I think to myself, I have every right to feel terrified, but right now this fear does not serve me. Once I'm done presenting, I give myself permission to feel as scared as I want. But for now, I need to put my head down and focus on the material that I know and the presentation that I've well-rehearsed."

"The other thing that helps is to try to have a sense of humor about the whole thing. After all, joy and laughter cannot occupy the same space as fear. This is why before a big speech I will often make fun of myself, the audience, my material... Then, I think about how silly it is for me to be afraid. And if I screw up on the stage, I smile and laugh and the audience smiles back. Remember, everyone knows that you're terrified. And they would be terrified too. But they see that you're trying. That you had the bravery to walk out on that stage. And that alone is more important than anything you could say in your speech."

Sabrina feeling much better picked up her que cards, "Okay, let me know what you think." After a deep breath she began, "Fellow classmates, I am here today to share a message of hope and optimism about our school's future…."

Since we fear the unknown, find bravery through preparation and mindfulness of all the glory that could be.

57 Our Fleeting Emotions

Arya called her parents and told them that she was dropping out of school. Her father calmly responded, "I know that you're unhappy, but are you certain of your decision? I mean, you've always done really well in school." "I am certain!" she replied. "I want to come home now!" "Okay," her father replied. "But before you do, you must do three things for me." "Anything, papa, I just want to come home." "You must finish this semester, while maintaining your grades. You must join at least one social or academic club, and you must agree to participate in at least one social event on campus every week." "Seriously! Why can't I just come home?"

"We've spent a lot of money for your classes, and it's important that you complete what you've started. I'm also concerned that your feelings may be misguided. That you're confusing your difficulty in making new friends with your enjoyment of learning." In a soft voice Arya responded, "Okay, I'll stay, but only until the semester is over?" "Good girl," he said to her with great relief.

Her father speaking to her on the phone at the end of the semester, "Well, do you still want to come home? Because if you do, we will book the flight today." "Are you crazy?" she responded. "I love this school. I have so many friends now. It was like you said papa, I was just feeling a little homesick."

I'm happy in this moment so my life is grand. I'm sad in the next, so it's all gone to hell. Our emotions ever fleeting, our perception of our reality, always changing.

58 BE MINDFUL OF YOUR THOUGHTS

Becky has been a nurse at the same hospital for ten years. Every night before she goes to bed, she prays for the same promotion. "Dear God, I have worked so hard at this job. I've served my time. I've shown my value. Please help me to get this promotion. You know that I deserve it. You know how much it would help my family."

Arriving at work the next day, Becky ran into Tammy her nemesis, and her primary competition for the job. "They'll probably promote her over me," she said to herself. "She's always kissing up to the managers. That's what stinks about this place. It has nothing to do with how hard you work, or how long you've been here. Just who you know, and who's your so-called friend."

Soon after, through her own unintentional manifestations, Becky lost the promotion to Tammy. "I don't understand," she said to herself, "I prayed for this promotion every single night. Why were my prayers ignored?"

Thoughts lead to feelings, feelings to vibrations, vibrations to manifestation. So, always be mindful of your thoughts. For your thoughts can often cancel out your prayers.

59 Focus on the Positives

"You don't understand, I used to make a lot more money at my other job, and I didn't have to put up with a boss who is a complete moron." Her friend responded, "You have a steady job that pays the bills, right?" "I guess," she replied, "but my other job was so much better." "Until you got laid off..." The woman rolled her eyes, "Yeah, until I got laid off."

Her friend continued, "Instead of always worrying about what you had in the past, you should be appreciate what you have right now. You have an excellent job with steady pay, and if you wanted to, you could really do well here." The woman nodded her head in agreement, "You're right, every time I think about my old job I just get upset. What's the point?"

It's impossible to manifest something positive when your focused on the negatives. It's impossible to move forward when your focused on the past.

If you must focus on the past, do so with a sense of appreciation for the lessons that you have learned and the experiences gained. Be appreciative of the journey completed and how it has made you into the person that you are today.

If you must focus on the future, do so with hope and anticipation, not fear and anxiety. For fearing the future brings no solutions to the present, only the increased likelihood that you will unintentionally manifest that which we fear.

60 Using Appreciation to Heal

Every day I would think about the stupid things that my friend had said to me over the last year. In the past we used to have normal conversations often finding common ground on most issues, but now it seemed like we lived in two different realities.

Admittedly, a part of me enjoyed our rigorous debates because I often felt that I would prove him wrong. But the reality is, these arguments were just draining and did little to sway either of our opinions. After a while, it didn't matter if I was right or wrong, I just wanted to be free of these bad feelings, and free of these endless arguments.

At first, I tried my usual arsenal of self-healing tools to work through my anger. I visualized putting bright light around my friend. I prayed for compassion and understanding. I tried to consider his side of the argument. I did everything that I could think of but nothing seemed to work. Then I decided to pull out the big guns and use the power of appreciation to heal.

I started to reflect upon all of the good times that we had throughout the years. How he had been so supportive in my times of need. How I truly loved the guy regardless of his many flaws. Then just like magic, the moment I focused on how much I appreciated him instead of how wrong he was, all of the anger, the endless arguments in my head, they all went away.

To heal we must put aside our anger, our desire to be right, and focus on the things that we appreciate.

Spiritual Well-Being

Don't just survive, embrace the opportunity, and thrive.

We are not meant to suffer the painful lessons of others.

As I teach, I continue to learn. As I give, I continue to grow.

Every act of cowardice comes with a lifetime of regret.

The more we avoid the pain, the greater it will be.

Hate is a gift that can be accepted or rejected. To accept it, is to take on its painful lesson. To reject it, is to hand the lesson back.

The path in life is not always clear. We are often misguided by our unhealthy habits, and in search for quick solutions. But if we continually test the waters and pay attention to the results, life will eventually guide us in the right direction.

The art of mastering positive change is to take several small steps, one day at a time.
Always act out of love. Love for yourself, and love for others.

When we sit in silence and calm our mind, all of the answers become clear.

Hell is a construct of our emotions, built brick by brick, by the limitations of our own fear.

We all know the truth, the right thing to do. Following through with our actions. Always selecting the righteous path. This is the challenge that we face every day. This is the test of our lives.

The reason that we are often so angry with others is because their behavior is a painful reflection of our own.

Each struggle, a necessary step for our growth.

The sooner we face our fears and tackle our challenges, the happier and more peaceful our life will be.

The only thing that matters about the past, is the person it has made you today.

Let go, appreciate your growth, and apply what you have learned. That is our mission in this life.

Never break the spirit of an aspiring soul. For even if they don't reach the top of the mountain, the attempt is all that matters.

Embrace your mistakes for each one is a gift. The more you pay attention, the easier the lesson will be.

The greatest gains are those made through small adjustments and broad measurements.

61 Walk Our Own Path

Mr. Lee had worked at his family business his whole life. He washed the dishes. He cooked. He hired and managed the staff, and now that his father had passed, he managed the books. There was no question about it, his father was his hero. He was the cornerstone of his family, and the rock that kept their business running through all of these years. But it wasn't until Mr. Lee took over the books that he realized just how much trouble the restaurant was in.

"Why didn't he tell me?" Mr. Lee said to his wife. "We could have helped. We could have done something to avoid this mess." "As Mrs. Lee stared into a pile of bills, "It was his ego. He would've rather have died than to face the embarrassment of his failure." "Well, that's exactly what happened, and now we're stuck cleaning up his mess!"

At first Mr. Lee, like his father, felt completely defeated. But then one day his wife said something profound, "You know I loved your father, but he was a very stubborn man. You always came to him with great ideas but he would never listen to you. So now, this is your chance. All of this is a blessing. Yes, your father has left you with nothing but a shell of a company, but now it's your shell. You can do things right now. Do things your way, the right way. And when it succeeds, and I know it will, it won't be because of your father. The victory, the success of this business, will be truly yours."

Mr. Lee never felt so inspired. He realized for the first time in his life that he was finally free from his father's shadow. Yes, it would mean that the business would have to file bankruptcy. That they would lose some staff and even some customers. But now he could truly rebuild, and in doing so, build something special. Something of his own.

It was a difficult couple of years, but before long Mr. and Ms. Lee's business was one of the most successful restaurants in the city. The paper called their menu, "Innovative! A blend of traditional and modern cuisine." Mr. Lee staring out at the packed restaurant with immense pride said to his loving wife, "I wish my father could see me now." Mrs. Lee warmly replied, "You know he can. And do you know what he would be most proud of?" "That we survived all of this?" "No. That you built something of your own. If we would've just taken over your fathers' business, then that's what it would have always been, your father's business. Instead, we built something of our own, something special and unique."

Don't just survive, embrace the opportunity, and thrive.

This is your life; treat it as such. Enjoy the free-will bestowed upon you and select your own path. Be assured, you will make many mistakes along the way, but in doing so, you will learn many profound and important lessons. So, take a step forward in whatever direction you choose, but no matter the path, make the journey your own.

62 The Law of Non-Interference

A father suffering through his son's addiction, "I'm releasing you now. I'm releasing you and this burden which is your drug addiction from my life. It's not that I don't love you. It's not that I've given up hope." The father leaning forward with tears in his eyes, "It's just too painful. It's too painful to watch you suffer through the same lessons. There is a part of me that wants to drag you back to that rehab center. To sit by your bed until you detox once again. But all that would do is to bring us back to this very same spot. I realize now that this is your lesson and your choice. So, I'm freeing you now. I'm freeing you to let you complete your journey, whatever that may be."

We are not meant to suffer the painful lessons of others.

It's often difficult to know at times if we're providing support to our loved ones or interfering in their soul's contract? There are many lessons that we must learn on our own. At what moment is the most loving act the act of letting go? It's the moment that we suffer needlessly for their lessons. It's when our actions cause more pain than good. It is when our help is continually refused.

Remember that their soul chose this painful lesson. Not to suffer but to grow. Regardless of our intentions, letting go can often be our most loving act.

63 Teacher or Student

A man shared with his wife his decision to no longer meet with his friend at the coffee shop. "Why not?" she asked. "I used to enjoy his company, I mean, no one has better stories about hunting and fishing than Tom, but now all he talks about is his crazy daughter and out of control grandkids." "I see, and you don't think that you can provide some helpful advice about his family?" "Trust me, I've tried, but he never listens." The wife responded with a look of concern on her face, "You've been friends with Tom for years, and like you said, you've learned a lot from the guy. Do want you want, but maybe it's your turn to be the teacher? Maybe it's time to give a little back and be a helpful shoulder to lean on?" The husband responded with a look of embarrassment, "As usual my love, you are right."

As I teach, I continue to learn. As I give, I continue to grow.

This Earth, this place of reincarnation, is our school. What is our purpose here? It is to experience, to learn and to grow. Who helps us along the way? God (source), our guardian angels, but most importantly, our soul group, each other. When considering if you want to continue a relationship with someone don't just ask, "Does this individual serve me?" Also ask, "Am I meant to serve them?" Remember in this life, you are either the teacher or the student. So, never miss the opportunity to teach to those who are ready to learn.

64 Stand Your Ground

A cowboy rode into a small town on his trusted horse. The streets looked abandoned as if everyone packed up and left in a hurry. As he neared the town center a man in a black vest slowly approached. "If you're passing through, you can keep going." "What happened here?" "Nothing for you to worry about." The man slapped the back of the cowboy's horse, "Go on now! There's nothing for you here."

As the cowboy continued through the town, he came upon an older couple sitting outside. "What happened here?" The couple sat in silence as they stared at the man still standing in the street. The cowboy then said to his horse, "Slow down, boy. Not sure we're ready to leave quite yet."

What the man in black didn't know, is that the cowboy had just come from a similar town. A town where he had lost everything including his wife and child. Now, for the cowboy, there was nothing left to lose. Nothing but the searing pain of loss that he carried in his heart. Nothing but the regret he carried for the day that he didn't fight back.

The cowboy sat still on his horse and stared at the man in black. He thought about everything that the man represented. He thought about how his life would be if he chose to move on. "You know what?" the cowboy said to his horse. "This place is starting to grow on me. Yep, I think this town will do just fine."

The cowboy secured his horse to a fencepost and started to walk toward the man. As he did, two other men stepped outside a salon with rifles in hand. The cowboy speaking to himself, "Every step that I've taken since I left my home, was a step that I regret. I don't think I have it in me to go any further. There's no point in living, if you're going to live your life like a beaten down dog. No point in building, if others are just going to take it away. This ends today. This ends now."

The cowboy spoke in a stern voice as he approached the men, "I've got good news... I've decided to stay." "Not here you won't," said one of the men as he cocked his rifle. "So, this is your town?" "That's right, and we choose who comes and goes." The cowboy looked around, "Well from the looks of it, everyone is gone." "That's not of your concern, now, is it?" The cowboy stared silently at the three men before he responded, "Well I recon... Now it is."

This is the first time that the men had faced any opposition. The other townsfolk had always cowered in fear. There was something different about the cowboy, something in his eyes. He wasn't just ready for a fight. He was hungry for one. He was hungry for redemption. Hungry to right a wrong. Hungry not to repeat the same mistake. The man in black took a step back and said, "Well, watch yourself around here. We'll be keeping an eye on you." The cowboy smiled knowing then the men's true spirit, "Okay then. I'll do the same."

Every act of cowardice comes with a lifetime of regret.

65 We Need to Feel in Order to Heal

Tonya received a devastating text from her boyfriend, "I think it would be best if we take a break..." The pain felt from his betrayal was too much to bear. She felt like she had invested her whole life into this man and all he can do in return was to send some cowardly text.

Tonya, in an attempt to distract herself from the pain, grabbed a carton of her favorite ice cream and started to flip through her phone. She texted her friends. She posted on social media. She ate a big bowl of her favorite ice cream. She poured herself a glass of wine. But no matter how much she tried to distract herself from the pain, it just wouldn't go away.

Tonya, visiting her family, sat outside on the deck and drank some tea. As she did, that old familiar feeling started to creep back in again. She immediately reached for her phone, but there was no service. She looked toward her parent's house, but new there was nothing good to eat or drink. With nothing else to do, she sat there in silence and felt the pain as it flowed through her body. After a moment of reflection, she finally realized, "I am so bored of thinking about Barry. That man has brought me nothing but pain. Maybe I just need to be by myself for a while..."

Sipping her tea, Tonya started to think of all the things that she wanted to do with her life. All of the things that would make her happy. As she did, that pain that she had been carrying for weeks, slowly and silently just slipped away.

The more we avoid the pain, the greater it will be.

66 They Don't Hate Me

A wife reading the comments of her husband's latest post on social media, "Boy, these people really hate you." "What do you mean?" he replied. "That post has over four thousand likes." "Yeah, and almost the same number of nasty comments."

The husband laughing responded, "These people don't know me well enough to hate me. They have no idea of my moral character or the life that I've lived." Shaking her head as she continued to read, "I don't know, this sure seems like hate to me." "They're not upset at me. They're upset because I've said something that they know is true. If I wrote, "The sky is green," no one would comment because there is no truth in that statement. They're responding because the truth is unsettling to them, and that's the point." "Yeah, but don't these nasty comments bother you?" Still laughing, "No, I appreciate everyone's enthusiastic response. If they're commenting, it means that they are paying attention, and if they are paying attention, it means that they're learning... At least I hope so."

Hate is a gift that can be accepted or rejected. To accept it, is to take on its painful lesson. To reject it, is to hand the lesson back.

We come to this Earth in search of the truth. The truth of who we are, of who we want to be. The truth has no sides, no political affiliation, no strict religious constructs. It is instead a piece of knowledge that resonates with our soul and guides us on our path of enlightenment.

67 The Process of Elimination

I woke up one morning hung over from a bottle of wine. "This has to stop," I said to myself. "I can't spend the rest of my life feeling this way." I kneeled down on the floor and began to pray, "Dear God, please help me end this destructive habit. It no longer serves me. It now only brings pain."

Later that day I reflected back to a conversation that I had with a girlfriend when I was much younger. I asked her, "Why do you drink every night? Can't you see how damaging it's been to your life. You've lost your driver's license, jobs, but you still keep drinking. Why?"

She replied, "I get up every morning and I feel fine, but right around the time I get off of work this physical pain comes into my chest. It has nothing to do with being sad or depressed. For me, its physical, not emotional. I'm in pain, and drinking is the only thing that I know that takes away the pain."

I completely related to what she was saying. If I drank too much one evening, the following evening I would have a similar pain in my chest. For me as well, this pain seemed more physical than emotional. With this in mind I thought, let's begin a process of elimination to figure out what is causing this physical pain, this chemical depression.

The first logical step of course was to completely stop drinking. Especially since the alcohol itself is a depressant and surely was contributing to my problem. And admittedly after I stopped drinking, I did feel much better. But eventually over time, this chemical depression returned.

I then considered other factors such as diet, sleep, exercise, and the medications that I was taking. I recalled having a similar reaction when I took prescription sleeping pills. Once I stopped taking the pills, this pain, similar to the one that I was feeling, immediately went away. I wasn't taking sleeping pills at the time, but I was taking an over-the-counter sleep aid. As an experiment, I stopped taking the PM pills and shortly after the pain in my heart and the desire to drink every night, immediately went away.

There was of course a lot more work that I had to do with forming new habits and how I delt with stress, but identifying this contributing factor was a big step towards helping me with my sobriety. And it all started through a process of elimination.

The path in life is not always clear. We are often misguided by our unhealthy habits, and in search for quick solutions. But if we continually test the waters and pay attention to the results, life will eventually guide us in the right direction.

The point of the story is in no way meant to diminish the destructive disease of alcoholism, or the extensive treatment needed by many. It is instead to say, if something is troubling you physically, it might be helpful to work through a process of elimination to identify what it is causing the pain. For me, this adjustment was one of the keys to my sobriety. For others I'm sure, it will be a much different path.

68 CHANGES THROUGH SUBSTITUTIONS

A few years ago, I was about thirty pounds overweight. I felt horrible, I looked horrible, and I was starting to accumulate a lengthy list of health-related problems. Then somehow, mostly through trial and error, I finally learned the trick of using small substitutions to slowly change my diet. I substituted a sugary desert every night for jello, and then eventually the jello for a bowl of fruit. I substituted salty chips for a pickle. Lemonade for lemon water. And then the big one, wine for light beer, and then eventually, beer for water. During this process, I never went hungry. I always ate as much as I wanted and whenever I wanted. To lose this weight, all that I had to do was to make small positive adjustments each day to my diet.

The art of mastering positive change is to take several small steps, one day at a time.

This same lesson applies to many aspects of our life. We're not meant to starve ourselves in anyway, and every choice for change does not have to be dramatic. Instead, we should all work toward small positive adjustments in our life. Easy adjustments taken one step at time, and one day at a time, slowly moving forward toward a better life.

69 THE KEY TO A LONG-TERM RELATIONSHIP

In celebrating our 20-year wedding anniversary, I asked myself, what is the key to a long and happy relationship, and what advice would I give to my children on their wedding day?

The first thing I would say is don't sweat the small stuff. We all have our little quirks, our odd behaviors, and strange habits. The worst thing that you can do is to try and change all the little intricacies about someone you love. The more you gripe and nitpick about who they are, the more you argue about stupid trivial things, the less chance your marriage will have to survive.

Secondly, have a sense of humor about yourself and about each other. If you do something stupid, own up to it, and if appropriate, laugh about it. You left the car in neutral and it rolled into the neighbor's fence, "What an idiot I am." Your spouse leaves the door wide open when they left for work, "There you go again, inviting all the criminals into our house." Marriage is not meant to be competition. It is a shared path, hopefully full of joy. So do your best to make the journey joyous. Have fun, laugh, and always keep a sense of humor.

Finally, always treat each other with dignity and respect. It doesn't matter who is right or wrong. It doesn't matter if you deserve to be angry. Remember, in every relationship there is always a point of no return. That one single act of violence. Those words that should have never been spoken. That utter act of selfishness. That's all it takes sometimes to end a long and happy relationship.

Always act out of love. Love for yourself, and love for others.

70 THE POWER OF SILENCE

The young woman began her five-hour drive home to see her mother. As she did, she scanned the radio hoping to find a good song. "Another commercial..." She pressed the scan button again, "I'm so sick of the news." Again, "I hate this song." After scanning one more time the woman abruptly turned off the radio, "Forget it! I'd rather sit in silence."

After a moment of stillness, she began to notice all of the sounds of the road around her. The rumbling beneath her feet. The swoosh of a car as it passed by. "I've never done this before," she said to herself. "I've never driven without listening to the radio." Noticing how relaxed her body felt, "You know what? This is kind of nice."

For the first hour of her drive, the woman struggled through her usual thoughts and concerns. But as the second hour approached, she found herself in state of peaceful reflection. She was no longer thinking about her struggles with her boyfriend or concerns about paying for school. Now that these worries had run their course, there was nothing left but peaceful silence and emotional contemplation.

With her mind finally at peace, she imagined her boyfriend by her side. Confused by her emotions she thought, "I feel nothing but pain when I think of him. Then, why am I with him?" And then she realized, "I spend all my time worrying about losing him. I never thought to ask if he even makes me happy." Then she pictured herself at school. And for the first time, it wasn't fear that she was feeling, it was her desire to finish. She realized how enthusiastic she was about becoming a nurse and how she didn't want anything to get in her way. "Why would I ever quit nursing school? What was I thinking?"

After more silence and reflection, "I've had everything in reverse. Every concerning thought, the opposite of what I actually desire. Now that I've put these worries aside, I finally realize what I truly want. I want to be free. Free to move on. Free to grow."

As the young woman pulled into the driveway, she was greeted by her mother, "How was your drive?" "So peaceful," the daughter replied. "I did the best thing ever." "What's that?" "I turned off the radio and spent the trip reflecting on my life." The daughter continued as she threw her bags upon the ground, "And do you know what? You were right. I need to take a break from Deven. And I need to do whatever it takes finish nursing school." The mother in tears responded, "I'm so glad to hear you say that. You're so close to finishing."

As the mother hugged her daughter she asked, "What changed your mind?" "I've spent all this time stubbornly justifying my choices instead of taking the time to consider how I actually feel." The mother shook her head in agreement as the daughter continued, "You know it's hard for me to admit when I'm wrong." "None of that matters now. What matters is that you're finally realizing what's important." The mother hugged her daughter again, "Oh honey, I'm so proud of you. You're going to make an amazing nurse."

When we sit in silence and calm our mind, all of the answers become clear.

71 It All Begins with Our Choices

Most consider Casandra to be a pessimist, but if you ask her, she'll say she's a "realist." That she has a realistic view of the world and that she knows her limitations. She has no interest in wild fantasies of things that will never manifest. "These "things" that people desire. They bring nothing but pain and disappointment." As a result, Casandra, through her own limited view, is destined to live a limited life. Happiness for her is rare and fleeting, and personal growth, almost nonexistent. In many ways, she has unknowingly created her own living hell. Her soul endlessly reincarnating onto this Earth, rarely learning new lessons, ever so slowly ascending within the spirit world.

Hell is a construct of our emotions, built brick by brick, by the limitations of our own fear.

There is a path out of this hell. Out of the fear that captures and controls us, and it begins with our thoughts. Our thoughts create our emotions, our emotions manifest our reality. What we believe, is what we are. For Casandra to free herself form her painful existence, she first must choose. Choose to believe that there is more to this life than simply just being. That there is a purpose, and a chosen path.

She must believe that there is more than just herself. That she is connected to this world, to the souls within it, and to the spirit world beyond. That life doesn't end at death, and that her soul is eternal. But most of all, she must decide that she is loved, that she is deserved, and that she is in control of her destiny.

72 Do What's Right

Coach Willson blew his whistle as the team gathered around. "Alright, settle down everyone. Excellent job today. Before the school year starts and our season begins, I want to talk to you about something important. It's a mindset of how to become a true champion. And that's what we are going to be this year, district champions." The boys cheered in agreement.

"All right, settle down. To become a true champion, not only on the field, but in your life, you have to embrace one simple philosophy... DO WHAT'S RIGHT." The coach stared in silence at the team. "I'm going to say it again. DO WHAT'S RIGHT. Sounds simple, right?" The coach shaking his head, "It's not. Everyone one of us is faced with temptations. I don't need to study today. I'll take it easy on the field. I'll try harder tomorrow. No one will know... DO WHAT'S RIGHT."

"Trust me. If you live by these words, if you embrace their meaning, it will change your life. You say to yourself, "I don't need to study today." Do what's right, study harder. "I'll take it easy on the field." Not today, not ever. "I'll try harder tomorrow." There is no tomorrow. DO WHAT'S RIGHT..."

"Remember, every choice you make in life, they all matter. They're all a big deal. Live by these words, and I promise you, you'll be champions on and off the field."

We all know the truth, the right thing to do. Following through with our actions. Always selecting the righteous path. This is the challenge that we face every day. This is the test of our lives.

73 Cancel Culture

Cindy and Jada were the two friends in the group that never got along. Some say this was due to petty jealously, others their competitive nature, but regardless the two rarely had an outing where they weren't at each other's throats.

Cindy, in a poor attempt at humor, posted a picture of Jada with a banana sitting in front of her. The caption read, "Look! Jada with her favorite breakfast!" The moment she posted the picture Cindy knew that she had made a huge mistake. But for some reason, out of spite or anger, she refused take the picture down. "It's not racist," she told herself. "It's just a joke. Anyway, she has said much worse things about me."

Cindy awoke the next morning with over a hundred notifications on her phone. "You're a racist pig!" "Nazi!" These where some of the more polite messages posted on her social media. Her friends feeling the pressure joined in as well. Some posted messages of solidarity for Jada, while others simply blocked Cindy's account. Cindy staring at her phone began to cry, "It was just a joke! Everyone who knows me, knows that I'm not a racist. I was just trying to be funny."

A few days later she finally soon took down the post, but it didn't matter. She had made a huge mistake, and now everyone, especially Jada, was piling on. "I can't believe you didn't see it before," Jada said to her friends. "She's a horrible person. We are all better off without her."

It was a long and painful month for Cindy but she had learned many important lessons. Lessons about her own cruel behavior and lessons about the meaning of true friendship. Feeling bad about the past, Cindy asked an old friend how things were with Jada. To her surprise her friend responded, "Jada!? We stopped hanging out with her weeks ago. We finally got sick of her trashing everyone." Cindy responded, "I guess that makes sense, but I've learned that we all make mistakes. Maybe I'll reach out and say hello?" Her friend replied, "Do want ever you want, we're done with her."

The reason that we are often so angry with others is because their behavior is a painful reflection of our own.

As we move with the herd, we often forget our responsibility to act as teachers and protectors. We forget that it's as easy to abandon, and so easy to be abandoned. Step away from a destructive soul if you must, but always do so with loving intentions and for the right reasons.

74 Life's Growing Pains

Diane had the worst year of her life. She got a divorce, crashed her car, and today she is attending her mother's funeral. Her friend, Maggie, who she hadn't seen for years, gave her a big hug. "I'm so sorry about your mother. She was a wonderful woman." Diane holding back her tears, shook her head and looked down at the ground. "I'm in town until Wednesday. Do you want to grab lunch tomorrow?" Diane with a smile replied, "That would be really nice."

The two girls met the next day at a café for lunch. After a bit of small talk Maggie politely asked about Diane's husband. "You don't know?" she replied. "We recently got divorced." "Oh, I'm so sorry. I didn't know." "That's okay. Trust me. It was for the better. I had no idea what a destructive force he was in my life."

As the conversation continued Maggie found herself inspired by Diane's story. And it wasn't because of her resiliency, it was because of her remarkable growth. "I know you've had the worst year of your life but I'm so proud of you. You're so strong now. I feel like I'm speaking to a different person. The last time we met you seemed so angry, so lost. But now you seem so confident and so in control of your life."

Each struggle, a necessary step for our growth.

75 That Could Be Me

Bradley a well-to-do businessperson walks past the same homeless man every day, and every day, he shakes his head in disgust. "Why the hell would I give him anything," he says to himself. "It would only encourage him to stay unemployed." Then one day, something profound happened to Bradley, he lost his job, and for a year he struggled to find new one. "What am I going to do?" he repeated to himself. "This is all that I know how to do. This is the only way I know to make a decent living."

Bradley eventually landed back on his feet, but his perspective of the world had changed. He realized now that nothing was guaranteed and that the universe did not owe him a certain standard of living. He also realized how fragile his financial situation was and how easy it is to find yourself penniless and on the street.

On his way to his new job, Bradley saw the same homeless man sitting in his usual spot. "How are you today?" he asked. "I hope you're staying warm?" Before giving the man any money, Bradley spent some time learning about his story. They discussed the choices he had made and the circumstances that led him to that very spot.

Over the next couple of weeks, Bradley would help the man, sometimes with money, and sometimes in other ways. One day his friend asked, "Why the hell are you helping that bum?" He quickly replied, "Because that was almost me."

76 Do The Difficult Stuff First

Olivia sat across from her friend Emma's office cubicle. They both shared the same customer service job but it was clear that Emma was struggling.

Olivia's always answered her phone within the first couple of rings. Her calls were short, polite and to the point. And as soon as the call ended, she would follow up immediately and continue to follow up until the matter was resolved.

Emma took a much different approach to her job. She would rarely answer her phone letting the complaint go directly to voicemail. It was often hours before she would return a call, and sometimes not even until the next day.

"What's the rush?" Emma asked her friend. "Our rules say we have 24 hours to return a call." "I take the call because the sooner I respond, the easier the call." "What!? How does it make the call any easier? An upset customer is an upset customer. What's the difference?" "It's true, all of these customers are upset, but the longer they wait, the more upset they're going to be.

Also, every second that I don't respond, is a second that I sit there worrying about some call that I have to make. For me, it's much easier to just take the call and get it over with. "Yeah, I guess that makes sense," Emma replied. "I'm just not as motivated as you, I guess."

Olivia rolled her chair over into Emma's cubicle, "I know and that's why I think that you've been struggling. Let me show you another trick that will make your life so much easier." Olivia pulled out a pad of paper and placed it in front of Emma. "Every day before work make a list of everyone that you have to call, every email that you have to send, and every task that you need to complete. Then put a check next to everything that you don't want to do, and two checks next to everything that you really don't want to do." "So put a check next to everything?" "Ha-ha, you're funny…"

"But here's the trick. Every day before you do anything, be sure to complete the double-checked items first and the single checked items second." "What?" Emma said as she pushed the pad away. "That's your advice?" "Trust me. If you do all the things that you dread first thing in the morning, then you'll have the rest of your day to relax." "Do you really do this?" "Yes! This way I don't have to spend my day worrying because all of the difficult stuff is already done."

The sooner we face our fears and tackle our challenges, the happier and more peaceful our life will be.

77 We Are Not Defined By our Past

Shelby always reflected on her past with a sense of regret. She didn't apply herself in school. She got mixed up the wrong crowed at an early age. And when drugs got into the picture, she made many, many, mistakes. Not a day goes by that she doesn't regret who she was in the past. So much so that the past, she feels, is what defines who she is today.

Sitting with a friend, "I was so stupid back then. I would do anything anyone would ask me to do. That's why I have to be so careful now. That's why I've decided it's better if I'm by myself." Her friend responded, "That's crazy." "The person you were when you were fifteen years old has nothing to do with the person you are now. For God's sake, we all do stupid things when we're young." "Yeah, but you don't understand. I can't risk making the same stupid mistakes again." "Why would you? You're a completely different person now?"

Shelby's friend leaned forward to make her point, "You know, you need to give yourself a break. You're one of the most responsible people that I know. If it wasn't for you constantly talking about crazy teenage years, I wouldn't have a clue that you ever had a wild side." Her friend, giving Shelby a hug, "From now on, no more talk about the past. All that I care about is who you are now. Okay?" Shelby wiped the tears from her eyes, "Yeah okay. You're right. You know, I wonder sometime if I use my past as an excuse to push people away." Her friend smiling, "Maybe so, sister, but I'm not going anywhere."

The only thing that matters about the past, is the person it has made you today.

The only question to consider when reflecting on our past, is have we learned our lessons? We weren't sent to this Earth to sit idle. We are not meant to be perfect. We didn't come here just to observe. In order to learn, we all must fail. For failure is often the only way to experience a lesson's true meaning.

So, the question remains, did Shelby learn her lessons? Since she has become a better person, we know the answer must be yes. But her constant regret does not serve her well.

The question she must ask now is not if she has failed, but what lessons has she learned. And then, how has she applied these lessons to her life? Only when her perspective shifts from the regrets of the past, to appreciation of the present, can she finally begin to heal.

Let go, appreciate your growth, and apply what you have learned. That is our mission in this life.

78 The Choice is Up to You

"I'm king of the world!" little Charlie yelled out as he ran across the room. "No, you're not!" his teacher yelled back. "I'm going to be president one day!" Charlie's mother shook her head, "No, honey. Only a few people get to be president and you clearly don't have the grades." "I can't wait to play football with the Eagles when I get older." "Not with that arm," his father replied. "And not unless you get a hell of a lot bigger."

"What's wrong?" his favorite uncle asked. "I don't know what I'm going to do with my life." "What? You're only ten years old. You have your whole life to figure that out." "Well, I can't be the president because I don't have the grades and I can't play with the Eagles because I'm too small." "Who told you that nonsense?" As Charlie kicked his football, "Everyone…"

"Well, I have some good news for you, Charlie, only you get to decide what you want to be in life." Charlie bashfully nodded his head while he stared at the ground. Seeing his disbelief, his uncle kneeled down, "I'm serious. You, and you alone, get to decide what you want to be. Not your teacher, not your parents, not me, only you, Charlie. Do you understand?" Charlie looked up at his uncle and began to smile. His uncle continued with a loud voice, "Who's going to rule the world? Charlie cheered back, "I am!" "That's right!" "Who's going to be president?" "I am!" "Right again! Remember, Charlie, you can do whatever you want. It's up to you."

Never break the spirit of an aspiring soul. For even if they don't reach the top of the mountain, the attempt is all that matters.

79 Embrace Your Mistakes

A young woman fell to the ground after she attempted to do a double somersault. "What are you doing?" her bother asked. "I'm speeding up my learning process." "By doing everything wrong?" "Exactly! The faster I learn what doesn't work, the faster I'll learn how to do it right." "What? As usual, sis, that makes absolutely no sense."

The sister continued in an attempt to educate her stubborn brother, "That's how you mastered that stupid video game of yours isn't it?" "No! It's because I practiced." "Sure, but you had to fail each level about a hundred times before you finally made it to the end." "Well yeah, but that's because it's a difficult game." So wouldn't you agree that the secret to mastering the game was to learn how to fail as quickly as possible?" "I mean… I guess." "And it wasn't until you learned everything that didn't work, that you'd finally got through each level." "Yeah, but that's not failing, its learning." "Exactly my point! I'm not out here failing. I'm out here learning." The brother bored with the conversation began to bike away, "Whatever. Still looks like failing to me."

Embrace your mistakes for each one is a gift. The more you pay attention, the easier the lesson will be.

80 The Temptation to Measure Daily

My mouth was wide open as I read one of the most idiotic emails that I'd ever received. It read, "I'm really worried. If you compare this week's sales to the same week last year, we our down 10%. This is a very concerning trend!" Shaking my head in shock and anger, I began to draft my response. "Are you serious? Who cares about one random week? We are up over 30% year-to-date. You should be happy, not concerned."

As angry as I was, I took a second to take a deep breath before I sent my email. Not because my response wasn't warranted but because I knew that it would do little to change the sender's perspective. We all make the mistake of measuring on a daily basis.

For example, every day I measure my weight on the scale. "Oops, I gained 2 pounds. I guess I shouldn't have eaten that desert." But the truth is the 2 pounds gained had little to do with the desert and more to do with my previous day's water intake. So, knowing this, why do I measure my weight on a daily basis? Why not once a week, or once a month? I do this because it provides for an opportunity to give myself a daily pep talk, "Great job!" or "Come on, you can do better."

When I thought about it, I realized that this was the same intention of the sender. It was not to scold me. It was simply his poor attempt to motivate me. So then, I thought, what would be the point of sending a snarky response? If anything, it would just make things worse.

So instead, knowing his true intentions, I responded with a much warmer email. "Interesting trend. I'll keep an eye on it. In the meanwhile, we'll keep working hard to make sure that we stay on track to have a record-breaking year. Up over 30% year-to-date. Not a bad start."

The greatest gains are those made through small adjustments and broad measurements.

When we try to manifest change, we must first choose our desired path and proclaim it to the universe. This is our expressed intentions.

The second step is to embrace the ideology of this thing that we want to become. We do this by slowly changing our thoughts, our feelings, our actions, and how we respond to the world. This is where we place our attention.

The last step is to let go and to believe. No grand gestures are needed. No dramatic changes. Just small adjustments made day by day to become the thing that we desire to be. This is how we are meant to receive.

Enlightenment

Sit in peace, and let the rushing waters take your troubles away.

So powerful is fear that it makes us co-creators in our own destruction. Shelter yourself from this fear by embracing the loving light within. Nothing is more powerful than God's light.

Nothing is by chance. There is no such thing as coincidence. Pay attention to the puzzle pieces. They may just save the day.

How do you want me to show you the way? Tell me the sign and I will put it in your path.

There it was, the answer to my prayers and the guidance that I needed, shown profoundly within the visions in my dreams.

Mass, substance, matter, these are all illusions in our life. Beautiful energy, controlled through our collective conscience, this is the truth of this world that we co-exist.

Even in your darkest hour, when the world is collapsing all around you, your angels are by your side always ready to help.

Our journey is personal one. The signs provided, customized to our specific needs. Guiding us each step of the way.

I guide you as I would myself, with great care and loving intent.

There is magic all around us. All we need to do is to pick up our wands and to start to practice.

You are the director of your life. Every thought, a line in your script. Every scene, yours to control.

Always pray for the truth to be reviled.

We all communicate through the collect conscience. Our mission, to find the truth. Our purpose, to grow and to evolve.

It's not the challenge that matters, it's the lesson learned.

Don't argue with crazy or stupid, you will lose every time.

I free you from my life. I do this not as an act of selfishness, but as an act of self-preservation, as an act of self-love.

The most destructive choices are the one's made out of anger.

Live pure in your intentions, for karma is a debt that will always be paid.

Stand independent in your choice and reason, and always act with a loving heart and loving intent.

81 Stay Peacefull in the Flowing Water

A great Indian chief met with his counsel to discuss the tribe's future. From the north, a scout had spotted a large caravan of Union Solders headed their way. To the south, their greatest adversary, the Comanches, had set camp blocking their escape.

The tribe's greatest warrior yelled out, "We shall fight!" "Fight who?" one of the council members replied. "Fight them all if we have to." "We should attempt to bargain," he replied. "Bargain with the devil? Or should we cower to our greatest enemy? Both of them would just as soon slit our throats." The tribe members nodded in agreement.

The tribe members looked to their chief. In a calm voice he replied, "I have prayed on this for many days. I have asked our descendants for wisdom and guidance, and they have spoken to me in my dreams." "What have they told you?" "Should we run?" "No! We should fight!" The chief remained calm, "Yes, we should prepare to defend ourselves…" Several of the members of the tribe cheered. "BUT… We will not be the ones to start this fight." The crowed grew silent. "We will ignore the white men to the north and we will avoid our enemy to the south."

"That's suicide!" the warrior yelled out. "We must act, or we will all die!" The chief stood up, "NO! We will not die! We will not be harmed. We will let these men flow around us like water on a stream." "We'll be trapped!" the warrior yelled out. "No," said the chief, "we are exactly where we should be. If we go to the north, or the south, we will only be jumping in the rushing waters. Instead, we will sit in peace and let our enemies find each other."

The chief raised his arms in the air, "I have prayed for many days. I have asked for guidance from our descendants. They have responded. Now, we must stay still and trust in the protection of our elders."

A few days later a winter storm blocked the mountain passage to the north. As a result, the Union Army was forced to take an alternative rout much further to the west. To make up for lost time, the solders headed back through empty planes to the south. "What was that?!" a solder yield out. "It's an arrow!" "It's the Comanches!"

Sit in peace, and let the rushing waters take your troubles away.

82 The Heavens Will Provide

One of my favorite stories is of a farmer who sat on top of his barn during a great flood. The first rescue boat arrived offering the man help and he replied, "Thank you my friend, but I have no doubt that God will take care of me." As the flood waters continued to rise, a second rescue boat appeared. The farmer yelled out, "Don't worry about me friend, go and rescue someone else. I've got God's loving protection on my side."

A few hours later the rushing water crested over the top of the barn and the man drowned. As his soul arrived at the gates of Heaven he asked, "Why didn't God protect me? Why did he let me drown?" The angel replied, "What do you mean? We sent you two rescue boats. Why did you refuse our help?"

How many times have you felt hopeless and alone, stuck in some horrible situation? Nobody seems to want to help. Nobody seems to care. In these moments it's easy to slip into despair. To ignore the help that is offered. We push it away out of pride. We assume that the cure is worse than the disease.

In these moments, give yourself one day. One day to cry out and scream. One day to feel sorry for yourself. One day to blame all of your problems on the world and the people around you. Really go for it and let it all out.

But once this day has passed, it's time to reset, to take stock, and to give appreciation. Consider then your options, the help at hand, and move forward with faith and conviction.

83 The Light Within

An evil witch cast her curse upon the small medieval town. Soon after the crops began to fail, and the townspeople began to grow ill. Everyone in the town was affected by the witch's spell except for little Elizabeth who was happy as she could be.

"Have you no fear," her father asked. "Fear of what?" she replied. "Fear of the curse that has been put upon this town and its people." "Heavens, no father. For grandmother has taught me about the light." "What light is this my child?" "The light within us. The light that protects us from all."

The father grabbed his daughter and asked out of fear, "Is this another form of witchery?" "No, father! It is the light of God that exists within us all. If we choose the light, it will protect us. If we choose the light, then nothing can harm us."

"How then do you use this light, my child?" "Grandmother taught me to close my eyes so that I could see the bright golden light that surrounds my heart." Pointing to her father's chest she asked, "Do you see it father?" "I'm trying my child." "Don't be afraid, for fear hides the light." As the father struggled, he shook his head. "No, my child, I still see nothing but darkness." "Then I will pray for you. I will pray for us all. With God's light we will be protected. With God's light, nothing in this world can harm us."

So powerful is fear that it makes us co-creators in our own destruction. Shelter yourself from this fear by embracing the loving light within. Nothing is more powerful than God's light.

84 Paying Attention to The Puzzle Pieces

Casandra reached through her window to pet the neighbor's cat. Ms. Johnson, the sweet elderly lady who lived above her, lets Mittens out every morning before she heads to the grocery store. On the subway ride to work, Casandra found herself oddly intrigued by a billboard promoting a medication that helps to ward off strokes. The billboard reminded her of a dream that she recently had of a fleet of ambulances surrounding her apartment building.

That evening when Casandra returned home, she noticed that Ms. Johnson was absent from her usual chair out front. "Something is wrong," she said to herself. "I just feel it." Casandra knocked on her neighbor's door but heard nothing but silence. Still concerned, she returned later that evening and knocked again. This time she heard a faint moan. "Oh my God!" she yelled. "Don't worry, Ms. Johnson. I'm calling the police."

The paramedics found Ms. Johnson paralyzed and laying on the floor. Casandra yelled out to them, "I think she had a stroke." The paramedic replied, "How do you know?" "Please check, I really think it was a stroke." As one paramedic looked at the other, "I think she's right." The other nodding his head, "Good call, lady! You might have just saved her life."

Nothing is by chance. There is no such thing as coincidence. Pay attention to the puzzle pieces. They may just save the day.

I love the part of a movie, usually near the end, when the main character flashes back and remembers all the significant puzzle pieces found along their journey. These pieces, always recalled in perfect timing, help the hero to escape a certain tragedy to save the day.

We are never alone in this life. We have at least one guardian angel who is with us through our entire journey. Even though they can't give us the answers, they are eager to help. This is why we must pay attention to signs. That piece of information shared by a friend in passing. That odd vision that makes no sense. That bizarre dream that must have some meaning. These are all important puzzle pieces handed to us by our angels to guide us along the way.

There is no such thing as a coincidence. If something feels meaningful, then we should assume that it's important. That's not to say that we should obsess about every little thing. Just set it aside, that helpful piece of information, to be used in perfect timing at some point in the future.

To receive this helpful guidance, we must first pay attention. I've asked many psychics how one can develop our own abilities. The most common response is that we must pay attention to our visions, dreams, and intuition. As we do, we will gain greater confidence and understanding to their meaning.

Once we realize how magical the universe actually is, life becomes a lot more fun. So, enjoy all the little signs. Appreciate the ability to use them to your advantage, and never be afraid to ask for clarification from your guides.

85 Interpreting the Signs

Lucia prayed for her brother Lucas' safe return. It had been over a month since his unit was deployed to a location in Afghanistan where all contact with the civilian world was prohibited. "My dear angels, please give me a sign that my brother Luca is safe and that he will be returning home soon. We are all so worried about him."

The next morning while having breakfast Lucia watched as a red cardinal flew and landed on the kitchen window. "Oh my God Mamma, I think that's a sign from my angels." "No Lucia," her mother responded. "Red cardinals are a sign that your past relatives are visiting you." "Do you think that means that Luca…" "No Lucia. It just means that Grandmamma and Grandpappa are watching over us." "How will I know Mamma? How will I know that my angels are giving me a sign that our Luca is safe?" "Well what sign did you ask for?" "I just prayed that they would show me a sign, any sign at all." The mother laughed. "I'm sure when your angels give you a sign, it will be very specific to your bother. And when you see it, you will know. You'll feel in your heart, that your brother is safe."

"But what do you think it will be Mamma? Repeating numbers, a feather, some kind of animal?" "Before you go to bed tonight pray for your angles to show specific sign regarding your brother. Something unusual and uncommon, like a white butterfly landing on your arm, or a red feather in your path. This way when you see it, you'll know."

That evening Lucia prayed for her angels to show her a cluster of brilliant red feathers. Red was her brother's favorite color. "That will be the sign," she prayed. "If I see the red feathers, then I'll know that my brother is safe."

The following evening on the way home from school Lucia passed by her favorite store. As she admired the decorations through the window, she spotted the most magnificent stuffed rooster sitting high upon a shelf. "So, beautiful," she said to herself. "Look at all those rich colors. Especially its beautiful red tail." A huge smile appeared on her face as she jumped into the air. "My brother! He's safe! Thank you, my angels. Thank you for showing me this beautiful rooster and its brilliant red feathers."

How do you want me to show you the way? Tell me the sign and I will put it in your path.

Once we start to pay attention, the signs from our angels will seem endless. To help in our communication, always remember to be specific in your prayers. Let them know what the different signs means to you and for what you will be on the lookout.

Also, to help in your communication, it's important to pay attention to how you feel when you see a sign. What do you think the sign means? What is your best guess? What's your intuition telling you? What would you angels want you to know? Remember, the more powerful the emotional response, the more important its meaning.

86 Answers Await You in Your Dreams

I was struggling with a decision if I should separate from a business partner of mine. On one hand, he had brought a few clever ideas to the table, but on the other, I felt like I was doing all the work for half of the profit. This was a crucial decision that I couldn't screw up. Once I asked to separate, there would be no going back.

That evening, I prayed before I went to bed, "Dear God, please speak to me in my dreams and guide to the best decision." Early the next morning, right before I woke, I had an incredible dream that me and my partner were standing in our own lawns but reaching across the sidewalk to shake hands. Right then it came to me, "I know exactly what to do." I realized from my dream that there was a perfect middle ground where we could officially separate as partners, but still work together as needed.

There it was, the answer to my prayers and the guidance that I needed, shown profoundly within the visions in my dreams.

If you ask any gifted psychic, they will tell you that we all have the ability to speak to God, our angles, and our higher soul. One way to access this guidance is through a state of meditation where we silence our mind and listen to our inner voice, our intuition. Another method is to pay attention to the imagery within our dreams. Whatever your psychic power may be, it all starts with asking and then paying attention to God's response.

87 Everything is Beautiful Energy

An astronaut looked down on the Earth in awe, "It's so massive, so beautiful." Just then a peanut M&M floated past his view. "It's amazing to think that if you took out all the space found within in an atom, the entire mass of the planet would fit inside this single M&M." The astronaut captured the candy in his mouth as it floated by, "All in this one delicious bite."

The station's science officer stared out the window besides him, "I know, it's an amazing optical illusion, isn't it?" "The Earth?" "No, matter. We can see it. We can feel it. We can measure it. But in reality, all of this stuff… it's all just beautiful energy. This is what I wish more people could understand." "What's that?" "That it's all just beautiful energy." Looking back down on the Earth, "Our planet is beautiful energy. We are beautiful energy…"

As the astronaut enjoyed another M&M, "Well how do we spread the word?" "We all have to stop thinking of everything in the physical sense. This stuff all around us. This is all just an illusion." "Ha! That would make a great slogan. Earth… It's just an illusion." Laughing at herself, the science officer replied, "Well it is." Pointing through the window, "Look at the Earth. Now take away all of the matter. What's left?" Enjoying his last M&M, "Delicious, beautiful, energy."

Mass, substance, matter, these are all illusions in our life. Beautiful energy, controlled through our collective conscience, this is the truth of this world that we co-exist.

88 Your Highest Protector

The captain's vision came slowly into focus as he laid still upon the cold observation deck floor. "What's happening?" The artificial intelligence from the spaceship responded, "We are under attack." The captain looked to his side to see his second in command laying on the floor beside him. A blast from outside the ship had cut through the bridge destroying several hibernation chambers and killing most of his senior crew. The captain spoke again with anger and tears in eyes, "Who's attacking us?" The AI responded, "The ship is unidentified. The south cargo door has been breached. Four intruders have boarded the ship. They are in the process of removing several of the hibernation chambers." "They're taking the crew?" "Affirmative."

The captain, slowly regaining his strength, pushed his body up-right so that he could pray. "God and angels, I need you more than ever. Please help me to protect this crew and this ship. Please guide me… Please show me the way."

The captain took several deep breaths attempting to wake his body from the long hibernation. After each breath, he sat in silence as he gathered his thoughts. "Gravity!" The AI responded, "Captain?" "I'm supposed to use the ships gravity. Move all of the ship's gravitational thrusters underneath the crew's hibernation chambers." "Please confirm?" "Do it now!"

The captain ran down the long corridor as sparks from the blast flew all around him. As he reached the door to the crew's chamber, he saw four large aliens in the process of disconnecting several hibernation chambers. Speaking softly, the captain looked up spoke to the ships AI, "Are the gravity thrusters in place?" "Yes, captain." "On my command increase the gravity in the crew's chamber to 100%." "Confirmed." The captain took a deep breath to prepare himself, "Now!"

The large aliens slammed to floor. The captain just outside of the gravitational pull, reached into a nearby locker and removed a blaster. The weapon immediately recognized the captain's handprint, turning green and arming itself. The aliens seeing the threat of the captain down the hall attempted to stand up. The captain, with no other options, seized the moment and fired four times.

The aliens were dead. His crew and ship were safe. Catching his breath, the captain spoke softly to himself, "Gravity. Thank you, my angels. Thank you for your guidance." As he continued to catch his breath, he shook his head in disbelief, "Gravity, who would have ever thought?"

Even in your darkest hour, when the world is collapsing all around you, your angels are by your side always ready to help.

89 Seeing Repeating Numbers

Peter was terrified. For the third day in a row, he saw the number 666. Today it was on a billboard. Yesterday, a house number, and the day before, someone's license plate. Speaking to himself out of concern, "Who would put 666 on their license plate? They must be some kind of devil worshiper. I keep seeing this number. I know it must be some kind of sign."

Peter spent the next few days worrying about this number and the inevitable dreadful event that was about to occur. But then... nothing. "You would have thought something would have happened by now. Who knows? Maybe I adjusted my behavior and dodged a bullet?"

Contemplating to himself, "It's funny now that I think about it. On the same days that I saw the number 666, I also saw my angel number 444, and my lucky number 777. I saw so many positive signs. Or who knows, maybe all this stuff is just by coincidence."

Our journey is a personal one. The signs provided, customized to our specific needs. Guiding us each step of the way.

I love to look for repeating numbers. My favorite being 444, 555, and 777. 444 for me means that my angels are by my side. 555 means that there is positive change ahead. 777 means that abundance and blessings are on the way.

Similar to Peter, I used to struggle with the number 666, especially if saw it repeated over a brief period of time. But slowly I started to realize, "What am I so scared about?"

Nothing bad actually happens when I see this number. Then I finally realized, like everything in life, it's not the number that matters, it's my interpretation of the number that counts.

In reality, there is no set universal meaning for any series of numbers. The meaning is truly up to you. For example, in China, 666 is a very lucky number and the number 6 can be interpreted as "smooth." So why do I have this negative view of the number 666? I believe it's nothing more than bad programing. My entire life I've been told that 666 is an evil number. That it represents Satan and the devil. But here's the thing, I don't believe in a devil. So why am I torturing myself, and manifesting negative events into my life, over something that I don't believe? It's because I've been programed to do so.

"From now on," I told my angels, "The number 666 means that an upcoming event in my life may seem negative at first, but in reality, it will be a tremendous blessing." I chose this meaning because from my experience, this has always seemed to happen. "So go ahead angels, show me this number all that you want. But when you do, please be aware of my new interpretation."

There are two important lessons to take away from Peter's story. The first is that we must be aware of the bad programing that we've all received. Every once in a while, ask yourself, "Is this what I actually believe, or just what I've been told?"

The second, is to be initiative-taking when working with your guardian angels. Let them know when you see a particular sign or vision that this is what it means to you. This way the lines of communication will be clear and understood.

90 The Disarming Power of Love

Rhonda's son, Brandon, is one of the most stubborn teenagers that you could ever meet. He refuses to clean his room, go to bed on time, to eat correctly... Whatever his mother asked, Brandon out of pure defiance will do the opposite. She has threatened him with endless punishments. She has tried to take away everything that he values. But the harder she tries to push him in the right direction, the more he pushes back.

Completely exhausted, Rhonda tried a different strategy. She approached Brandon from a position of compassion and love. "Brandon, you know that I love you right." "Yeah." "What makes me sad is that you don't love yourself." "What do you mean?" "Everything that you do, every choice that you make, is leading you to a life that will be filled with pain and suffering." Brandon pushing her away, "Whatever! You don't know." "I do know, and do you know what, you know too. You're not stupid. You are actually quite smart when you want to be, and that's what you need to be now, smart."

Brandon continued to sit stubbornly in silence. "You think that I yell at you just because I'm trying to control you?" "Exactly!" he replied. "No, Brandon. It's because I love you, and I believe in you, and I want you to succeed. It's because I want you to have the freedom to do whatever you want with your life." "That's what I'm doing!"

"Yeah, I know. But what you don't realize is that the 15-year-old Brandon is crushing the hopes and dreams of 30- year-old Brandon. 15-year-old Brandon is forcing 30-year-old to have a bad job, to live in a run-down house, to struggle to pay the bills." "How do you know?" "You see the men around you, don't you? You know that they made the same choices that you're making now." Rhonda continued as Brandon rolled his eyes, "Seriously, Brandon. Look around you. Look at these men's lives. You know what I'm saying is true."

"The difference is that you still have a choice. They made their choice a long time ago. And just like you, they took the easy path every time. They didn't care about their grades. They didn't care about anything except having a fun time and look at them now. Is this the life you want? Because that is not a happy one. It's not a life that's filled with freedom and choice." Rhonda continued in a softer voice, "Don't trust me, Brandon. You go ask them yourself. They'll tell you."

Brandon with a tear in his eye stormed away from the table. His mother's message was finally heard. A message that was shared without threats or punishment, but instead, only loving concern about his path ahead.

I guide you as I would myself, with great care and loving intent.

91 Opening Your Third Eye

When Sasha was a baby, she had an amazing gift. Not a day would go by where her mother didn't catch her smiling off into space or joyfully playing with her imaginary friend. Out of the blue, she would tell her family things about their past or warn them about concerning events to come. It didn't take long for her parents to pay attention. If Shasha said not to drive the car that evening, you better believed that their family stayed home.

As the years passed, Shasha's gifts began to fade, and in many ways her parents were relieved. They didn't want their daughter to be thought of as different. So, they discouraged, and often ignored, her abilities the best that they could. By the time Shasha became a teenager, her gifts were long gone. That was until that fateful day when she spoke to her grandmother.

"Nanna, auntie says that you have psychic abilities, is that true?" "Yes, child, but we all of these gifts." "Not me, I've never predicted anything." "Ha! Is that so? You were actually quite gifted when you were a child. You just don't remember." "I was?" "Yes, you used to visit with your Pappa all the time." "Pappa who died?" "Yes. You would play with him and many other spirits almost every day." "I don't remember that. What happened?" "Our gifts are like anything in life, if we don't use them, they begin to fade." Nanna reaching over to pat Shasha on the head, "Don't worry child, your gifts, they're all still there."

Shasha intrigued by her grandmother's response, "So, you can predict the future?" "I have strong intuition at times, but I don't think this is my gift. For me, it's more about sensing the energy around me. Sensing peace when everything is safe and heavy vibrations when things are not." "I have that feeling sometimes." "I bet you do." "So how do I get these powers back?" "You mean how do you open your third eye?" "Yeah, Nanna, how?"

Shasha's grandmother responding with a warm smile, "Well, child, you're already on your way. Now that you know that you have these gifts, it's up to you to bring them out." "Yeah, how do I that?" "It's like learning how to play a piano. It's not going to come all at once. You have to practice every day, and then little by little, and it will all start to come." "Yeah, but how Nanna?" "By paying attention. By calming your mind and finding peace in your heart. By believing."

Nanna grabbed a coin from a nearby jar and placed it under a coffee mug. "Tell me child, what kind of coin is underneath this cup?" Before Shasha could answer, her grandmother put her hand over her mouth. "Wait... Don't just guess. The universe hasn't told you anything yet." Shasha sat back in her chair and impatiently stared at the cup. "Close your eyes... Relax... Clear you mind... Focus on your breathing, nothing else... Now put your thoughts aside and tell me what you feel. Does it feel like a penny? A nickel? Maybe a quarter?" "I'm trying, Nanna, but I don't feel anything." "Don't try so hard. Just relax."

Sasha, doing her best to relax, "It's definitely not a penny. It seems bigger. It feels like it's silver. I would say a quarter, but... that doesn't feel right either. It feels different. It's something else." The grandmother lifts the cup exposing an Italian coin pressed in silver and coper. "See! You were right." Shasha doing her best to agree, "Kind of, I guess."

Nanna placing her loving hand on Shasha's shoulder, "Anyway, it's not the outcome that matters, it's the exercise. Developing your gift, no matter what you believe, has little to do with predictions and everything to do with your feelings. Anyway, predictions are just guess-work and trust me, your mind will try to play tricks on you every time. What's important, is that you relax. You clear your mind and pay attention to how you feel. Do this, and everything else will come.

There is magic all around us. All we need to do is to pick up our wands and to start to practice.

Knowing that we are all gifted, we must ask ourselves; will we choose to develop these amazing gifts or will we remain blind to our own abilities? If you wish, express to your angels your interest in opening your third eye. Practice by finding peace through meditation and prayer. Be mindful of your emotions and trust in your intuition. It's all there waiting for you. Your magic. Your gifts. Your abilities. They've never left you. All you need to do is to practice.

92 You Are the Director of Your Life

"And... Action!" "Don't leave me baby. You know that I.... line?" "Cut!" the director yelled as he stormed toward the actor. "Are you kidding me? First you show no passion. Now you can't even remember your lines?" The actor embarrassed replied, "I'm sorry, I got distracted. I'll get it this time, I promise." "Okay, but this time, say it with passion. Remember, you love this woman and your about to lose her." The director settled back in his chair, "And... Action!"

"Don't... leave me baby." "What!? Cut, cut, cut." The director throwing his clipboard to the ground "That's a wrap. I'm done with this scene." "What do you mean?" the actor replied. "I can do it. Just give me one more chance." "No, I never liked this scene anyway. If anything, you just proved to me why it doesn't work. Your character just ends up leaving her in the next scene anyway, so what's the point?" "That's what I never understood." "Don't worry. We'll rework the script and shoot it again tomorrow."

You are the director of your life. Every thought, a line in your script. Every scene, yours to control.

Take control of your life. Be mindful of your thoughts and be mindful of your emotions. Remember, you are the director of your life. The quality and content of your life's story, your movie, is in your control. Don't like the script? Rewrite it. The scene makes no sense. Cut it out. The character doesn't fit. Remove them and recast. This is your movie, so be the director and take control.

93 Always Pray for the Truth

Frank and David's partnership just ended in the worst way. Their profitable company, which had excelled for years, all of sudden went bankrupt. Frank, in shock to his company's sudden collapse, dug through the books. "Where did all of these losses come from? There's something not right here." He knew in his gut that his partner, David, had been dishonest, but no matter how much he searched, the books all seemed correct.

Frank went to his attorney, "I know this guy is crooked," he said. "I just need you to help me prove it." But the attorney was of little help. "How am I supposed to help? You have no evidence of any wrongdoing. If anything, you appear to be as guilty as your partner."

That night Frank prayed to his guardian angels, "All that I ask is for the truth to be revealed." The next morning when Frank awoke, two simple words were stuck in his head, PAPER TRAIL. "Paper trail? Yes, I get it, but I don't even know where to begin." Staring up at the ceiling Frank prayed again, "I understand, I need to show a paper tail, but I have no idea where to look. Please guide me. Please show me the way."

The next morning Frank woke with two different words in his head, "YOUR CUSTOMERS." "What?" he said to himself. "That makes no sense. What would my customer records show?" But then it came to him, "They would show if our records were correct. It would show if my partner was lying. That's it! I need to establish a paper trail with my customers."

Frank immediately wrote all of his suppliers requesting a copy of their purchase records. Most of the companies immediately replied, and everything seemed on the up and up. But oddly, one company did not respond, and by chance, it was their largest supplier. Frank sent another letter, yet... still no reply. "This is really odd," he thought. "It's to their advantage to share these records. There's clearly something fishy going on here."

A month later the purchase records were subpoenaed by the courts, and just as Franked believed, the truth was all there. His partner had cooked the books, their largest supplier, equally involved. The truth of Frank's innocence was finally revealed.

Always pray for the truth to be reviled.

The truth is always your most powerful ally and greatest defense. Frank didn't pray for his partner's demise. He didn't wish upon him any particular form of justice. He left all of that up to their own karma. Instead, he prayed for the truth to be revealed. A simple prayer, so justified, so righteous in its request, that it would be impossible for the universe to deny.

94 Sharing the Truth

Two aliens looked down at the Earth from their mother ship. The year was 1973. "They have no interest in the truth. When we share our knowledge, they abuse it. When we warn them of their future, they ignore us." "Yes, but our mistake was in our approach." "Please explain." "Let's assume that the dominant species on Earth was the lion." "Continue." "What would happen if we approached the lion with our hand extended in friendship?" "It would surely eat us." "Correct. But why?" "Because it's their nature to do so." "So, what is mankind's nature?" After pondering the question, the alien responded, "Unique to this species, the answer varies greatly by the individual." "Agreed. For us to have assumed unanimity with humankind, that they were all the same, this was our mistake."

After a moment of silent contemplation, "So, to be effective in our intent, we must share our knowledge with the masses instead of the individual leaders." "Agreed." "To do this we must first share a technology that will allow one individual to express itself freely to another." "Yes, a web of information that can be accessed by every individual around the world." The two aliens nodded in agreement. "Then this is what we will do. We will share with them this technology first. Then we will slowly disseminate the truth through the masses."

We all communicate through the collect conscience. Our mission, to find the truth. Our purpose, to grow and to evolve.

95 Our Greatest Teachers

"Hey loser, eating by yourself again?" The two boys ran away laughing while the other sat alone with his lunch. "What the hell did I ever to do them?"

As the boy grew into a man, the lessons taught to him by the two bullies became profound. They taught him not only about resilience and personal strength, but also about compassion and the importance of treating others well.

Years later the man ran into the bullies at a school reunion. He politely smiled, feeling happy and at peace, while the two men tried their best to belittle him. "Still stuck at this school, I see." "Too afraid to make it in the real world?" "Yes," the man replied, "I've been the principal here for five years now.

Putting his hand on one of the men's shoulders, "In many ways I have you two to thank." "What!?" one of the men said loudly as he spilled his drink on the other. "Absolutely. You both taught me a lot. For example, our school has a no bullying policy and a place to go if anyone harasses them." One of the men rolled his eyes and shrugged his shoulders in embarrassment. "It's funny. Now that I think about it, you really helped to make me a better principal. So, thank you." The other man, drunk and hardly paying attention, put his arm around the principal and said in a slurred voice, "You're welcome." The principal laughing at the man, shook his head and walked away.

It's not the challenge that matters, it's the lesson learned.

96 Wanting Others to Behave

My son was complaining to me about a bully at school and wanted to know if he had permission to get in a fight if the trouble persisted. His natural tendency was not toward violence, but the kid's behavior had become intolerable and my son didn't know what to do. I said to him, "If I could only teach you one lesson, one lesson that would remove the vast majority of the emotional pain that you will have in your life, it would be to not worry about the behaviors and actions of others."

Sitting by his side, "If you like, we can certainly go through the pros and cons of having a fight, but what's important is that you take control of your feelings." Rolling his eyes in the air, "So, no to the fight?" Laughing as I put my arm around him, "No, you can't get into a fight, but the reason why is what's important."

"During your whole life, you are going to be faced with people who upset you. People will insult you and treat you with disrespect. They will lie to you. They will cheat and steal from you... Each time that this happens you will be faced with a choice of how you respond and how you feel. The question is, do you want to spend your life acting as the victim?"

My son staring at me with a look of confusion on his face, "So, how does this make this kid stop bothering me?" "If you choose to play the role of the victim, then all that you have to do is continue to let his behavior upset you. If you choose this path then he's already won, but... he's won by your choice.

If you choose to ignore his behavior, to laugh it off, to rise above it, then you've already won before the fight has even begun. Either way, win or lose, victor or victim, the choice is up to you." My son still with a look of confusion on face, "So, how do I get this kid to stop bothering me?"

"If he makes a joke about you, laugh it off and walk away. If he insults you, shrug your shoulders and move on. But if he touches you, or if her hurts you physically in anyway, then tell a teacher right away. Then when you get home, tell me right away. The point is not to let someone physically abuse you, but for you to stay in control of your emotions. For you not to react. The less you react, the less interesting you are as a potential victim. The less you react, the more inclined he will be to move on.

Don't argue with crazy or stupid, you will lose every time.

A significant percentage of the emotional pain that we suffer in this life is in the wanting of others to behave differently. To free yourself of this pain, stop carrying what others think, say, or do. Remember, there actions are never personal, and are only a reflection of their own inner struggles. Show sympathy toward this inner struggle versus anger, compassion instead of fear. The choice to play the victim is yours alone. The emotional response shared, a gift that only you can give.

97 Does This Still Serve Me?

Gail looked across at her friend Tammy who's just spent the last hour complaining about her life. "Why am I still friends with this woman?" she asked herself. "She brings nothing but stress and drama into my life. Why am I wasting my time listening to her endlessly complain?"

I free you from my life. I do this not as an act of selfishness, but as an act of self-preservation, as an act of self-love.

It's helpful on occasion to remember our purpose here on Earth. It is to grow, to learn and to experience. To learn from our choices, and to learn from the choices of others. So, Gail should consider; What lessons is she learning from Tammy? Is Tammy learning anything from her? Does this relationship still serve her? If not, there is no crime in stepping away from an unhealthy friendship. To the contrary, Gail releasing Tammy from her life, is in affect an act of love for herself.

So, how does Gail end her long friendship with Tammy without causing a ton of unnecessary pain and drama? The answer is with loving intent. She can start by speaking to Tammy's soul through her prayers and dreams. Letting her know that she is ripping up her souls' contract and releasing her from her life. As she does this, she sends Tammy positive energy and thoughts while placing bright light around her. Then when the friends actually speak, we hope that Tammy will receive Gail's loving message with understanding and dignity. But if not, this will be Tammy's lesson to learn, not Gail's.

98 Choose with a Peaceful Heart

Tyson is so angry with his brother. It seems like every day he does something stupid to destroy his life, and once again, he's being called to his rescue. Part of him wants to leave him there in the jail cell to rot. "Why should I bail him out again? How's he ever going to learn?"

Tyson blinded with anger, turned his car around, "Screw this and screw him, I'm going home." For several miles, his anger continued to fester, but eventually it began to fade. "I just don't know what to do," he calmly said to himself. "God, please tell me what to do."

Seeing a rest stop ahead, he pulled his car over and parked. Tyson punched his steering wheel several times before taking a few deep breaths. Exhausted, he sat in silence and stared out into the field ahead. After a while, his anger began to fade. He prayed again, this time from a place of peace, "God, please tell me what I should do. I just don't know what to do." After a long moment of silence, a voice, not heard in his head but down deep in his heart, responded, "Go free your brother."

The most destructive choices are the one's made out of anger.

Important decisions should only be made with a clear mind and a peaceful heart. When you're upset, stop, relax, and take a deep breath. Once your mind is empty and your heart is at peace, then the right decision will always come.

99 The Power of Innocence

A famous inspector is followed down a dark alley by his apprentice. "What's the first thing we will do once we arrive?" "We will gather the facts. We will review the evidence. We will gain an understanding of the characters involved. And then, once everything is laid out…" "We will know who's guilty?" "Possibly, or at least we will know who's a likely suspect."

"Do you always know your suspects right away?" "Not always. Not a first. But the more you dig, the more the guilty ones stand out." "You mean, the person who committed the crime?" "Not just them, anyone who is guilty. It's our human nature, you see. Guilt, shame, fear… these are all emotions that are hard to hide. All you have to do is to keep digging and the guilty will expose their fear every time."

"And what about those who are innocent?" "The most powerful defense that you can have, is to maintain a life of true innocence." "But don't the innocent get convicted?" "On occasion, but that's only if the investigator is lazy or corrupt. In most cases, one's innocence is always their greatest defense."

The inspector continued, "There was a case recently where a wife was murdered in her home. And as you would expect, the husband was one of the primary suspects. And what made matters worse, is that he couldn't produce a single alibi." "So, how did he prove his innocence?" "Well, that's the thing. He didn't have to, because there was no evidence to show that he was guilty. Not for the murder of his wife. Not of any crime."

"A year earlier, I had a similar case where the husband was the suspect." "Did they find any evidence on him?" "No, not directly, but the man lived the life of a guilty man. He was a gambler and womanizer. And there were rumors that he would hit his wife when he drank too much." "He sounds guilty to me." "And that's what everyone thought. And that's certainly how the man was treated. But guess what?" "He didn't do it?" "That's right. The evidence showed it was the woman's lover who was the killer, not the husband."

The inspector stopped at the edge of the alley to make his point, "Do you see the lesson in all of this?" "Don't assume someone is guilty just because they appear to be?" "That certainty was the lesson for the officers. But the husband, he had a lesson as well." "That if you act like a monster, everyone will automatically assume you're guilty?" The inspector laughed, "You're, close."

"That our actions have consequences and that karma rarely takes a straight path. If you steal a dollar from a man, it doesn't mean a dollar will be stolen from you. It means that you'll have to face a lesson regarding loss. If you abuse your wife, it may not mean that you'll be abused. But instead that she might allow herself to be abused by others." "We reap what we sow," the apprentice said as he reflected upon the lesson. "Exactly, my young apprentice. But also... a life of innocence is always your greatest defense."

Live pure in your intentions, for karma is a debt that will always be paid.

100 THE LESSON OF A SAMURAI

A samurai worrier stood victorious over a pile of dead bodies. He has spent his whole life preparing for this moment. He mastered his swordsmanship. He hardened his resolve. There was little thought taken in his actions. Once the enemy attacked there was nothing left to do but to kill. And so, he did, with perfect execution, and with little emotion.

As he stood there drenched in blood, the samurai noticed a man beneath him suffering in his last breaths. The man looked up with great fear, "Why?" The samurai looked back with great anger, "Why!?" He thought to himself, what a ridiculous question. The samurai responded in a loud voice, "Because you attacked my village! That's why!" Then with a final blow, the samurai struck the man with his sword.

Several weeks had passed since the village was attacked and not a day would go by that the samurai didn't think about the dying man. "Why do you continue to haunt me? You know that I was justified in my actions. You would have done the same to defend your village." But just then, as soon as these words were spoken aloud, he remembered. It was just year ago that he and his men crossed the border to attack a small outpost. It wasn't a village. No women or children were harmed. But still, it was an aggressive attack and many lives were lost.

"Why?" the samurai asked himself. "Why did we cross the border? Why did we bring this destruction to our village?" He realized then the true meaning of the dying man's question. Why is all of this pain necessary? No matter how many victories they had won. No matter how many lives taken. All this fighting, it has brought nothing but pain."

Years later the samurai inherited his place as the leader of his village. He had watched how his father had stubbornly led his people into endless wars. He was determined not to make the same mistake. "It's time for change," he declared. "From this moment forward, we will strive to have peace with our neighbors. For I never want to be asked again the question to which there is no answer... why? Why the needless suffering?"

To what purpose do we take this action? Toward what benefit do we make this choice? We must always ask ourselves, why.

We can always justify our actions, especially when we follow the pack. We do this because we believe it's expected. We do this, often with little consideration, simply because we are told it's right. But before we act, we should first consider; Why? Is this truly for the greater good? Is it done with loving intent? Is it independent from the expectation of others? If the roles were reversed, would we do the same?

Stand independent in your choice and reason, and always act with a loving heart and loving intent.

The End

100 Short Stories and Spiritual Lessons is the 2nd book by author Todd Knight and follows the highly rated book TRUTH SEEKER: Spiritual Knowledge Shared by a Gifted Psychic and Her Guardian Angles.

Copyright 2021, Knight Publishing, LLC / authortknight@gmail.com